Navigating Words: A Step-by-Step Guide to Natural Language Processing

Rachel Capper

Published by Rachel Capper, 2024.

While every precaution has been taken in the preparation of this book, the publisher assumes no responsibility for errors or omissions, or for damages resulting from the use of the information contained herein.

NAVIGATING WORDS: A STEP-BY-STEP GUIDE TO NATURAL LANGUAGE PROCESSING

First edition. March 24, 2024.

ISBN: 979-8224881307

Written by Rachel Capper.

Table of Contents

Chapter 1: Embarking on the NLP Journey

1.1 Setting Sail: Introduction to the Linguistic Frontier

Huddled in a small study, illuminated by cascades of lamplight, Sarah was determined to delve into the mysterious world of Natural Language Processing (NLP). The dusty room, bearing a collection of musty books and arcane symbols etched across the walls, had become her sanctuary as she embarked on a journey through the uncharted territories of computational linguistics. With her mind a blank canvas, she yearned to explore the vast potential of NLP and understand its wondrous applications.

NLP, the field that melds language and machines, fascinated Sarah, evoking visions of a future where humans and computers seamlessly intertwine. As she leafed through weathered textbooks flanked by crimson anatomy diagrams and ancient texts, her desire to comprehend the complexities of this frontier grew. Sarah was drawn to the intricacies of language, its various forms, dialects, and subtle nuances.

Utilizing an inquisitive mind and deftly crafted Google-fu, she began positioned snippets of information: introductory courses, research papers, blog posts, and library shelves filled with literary compendiums dedicated to computational linguistics. She yearned to forge her own path through the Linguistic Frontier.

Mesmerized by the common thread that intertwines humanity—the vast experience of communication—Sarah understood that NLP realized humanity's dreams of creating intelligent systems capable of perceiving the subtleties of language and understanding its true intent. This realization fueled her determination to understand and harness this revolutionary technology.

Surveying the landscape set before her, Sarah encountered the works of pioneers in the field, including Noam Chomsky, who redefined linguistic theory, and Daniel Jurafsky, who bared the essence of NLP's practical applications. These visionary sages had laid the foundation upon which NLP now stood, the ground fertile for a new generation of learners.

Arming herself with a trusty text-to-speech engine, Sarah listened to lectures, podcast interviews, and industry experts' testimonials. Each audio file beckoned her deeper into the expanding horizons of NLP: uncovering sentiment analysis, exploring part-of-speech tagging, and discerning the hidden patterns in vast collections of textual data. The knowledge she sought to acquire drew her deeper into a realm where machines tinkered with language and algorithms mastered the art of interpretation.

Unwilling to confine herself to standard references, Sarah peered beyond the traditional corridors of learning. She discovered online communities brimming with curated datasets, ranging from poetic lyrics to medical forums. Armed with theoretical foundations and numerical acuity, she foraged through unexplored islands of data to nurture innovation and invention, eager to buoy her understanding of NLP's capabilities.

Through this nonlinear and multifaceted learning process, Sarah realized that NLP was not mere processing of language; it represented an intricate dance, where technology sought to understand and mimic the dazzling array of human speech. She gained insight into the challenges posed by connotations, idioms, and cultural referents that weave through conversations, thereby prompting an exploration of cross-cultural considerations.

As dawn broke following several months devoted to this enthralling expedition, Sarah recognized that her preliminary knowledge had laid solid groundwork for her initial step on the Linguistic Frontier. But this was merely the tip of an iceberg—a world so vast, teeming with potential, that these meager beginnings could only serve as fuel to steer her onward. The journey into NLP required an insatiable hunger for knowledge and an eternal longing to unravel language, laced with dedication and persistence.

Eyes shimmering with determination, Sarah secured her research notes and ventured forth, ready to sail among the brilliant minds pushing the boundaries of NLP. The road ahead was dazzling and arduous—unpredictable yet bewitching—as she embarks on her expedition toward mastery, forever transformed by the enigmatic world of Natural Language Processing.

1.2 Trailblazers and Tales: A Historical Prelude

The field of Natural Language Processing (NLP) had humble beginnings, dating back to the mid-20th century when researchers embarked on a quest to teach machines the nuances of human language. This chapter, "Trailblazers and Tales: A Historical Prelude," sets the stage for understanding the origins of NLP and the pioneers who paved the way for its advancements.

To comprehend the advancements in NLP, it is essential to explore the challenges that researchers faced throughout history. The intricacies hidden within human language, characterized by its contextual richness, idiomatic expressions, sarcasm, and ambiguity, presented formidable obstacles for creating intelligent computational models. However, the progress made stands testament to the resilience and passion of the early NLP pioneers.

The story begins in the 1950s, with the birth of the computer age, when visionaries proposed the possibility of machine translation—automatically converting text from one language to another. This idea, sparked partly by the geopolitical tensions of the time, captured the imagination of scientists who saw the potential for enabling intercultural communication and breaking down barriers.

One of the trailblazers in machine translation was Warren Weaver, an American mathematician and scientist. In 1949, Weaver published a groundbreaking memorandum titled "Translation" that discussed the possibilities, challenges, and potential methods to automate language translation. His work paved the way for subsequent efforts, laying the groundwork for modern NLP.

Among the early successes in NLP was the Georgetown experiment, carried out by researchers at Georgetown University in 1954. Running on the world's first electronic computer, the IBM 701, the experiment aimed to translate

Russian sentences into English. Although the output was far from perfect, this experiment marked a significant milestone—demonstrating that machine translation could indeed produce intelligible results.

Over the next few decades, the NLP community witnessed a synthesis of techniques from linguistics, mathematics, information theory, and computer science. As computing power improved and new algorithms were developed, researchers focused on various aspects of language processing. Familiarizing machines with syntax, semantics, and pragmatics became crucial milestones, guiding the NLP field toward its goal of providing machines with an ability to understand, generate, and respond to natural language.

In the late 20th century, NLP faced a seismic shift with the adoption of statistical models and machine learning techniques. Instead of hand-crafting linguistic rules, researchers began leveraging large amounts of data to automatically learn patterns, perform language analysis, and even build conversational agents. This data-driven revolution unleashed a new wave of possibilities, propelling NLP into a new era.

While this chapter barely scratches the surface of NLP's historical tapestry, it highlights the remarkable efforts and milestones achieved by early researchers who were driven by an insatiable curiosity to create intelligent machines capable of understanding human language.

Embarking on a journey to understand the historical development of NLP will equip beginners with valuable insights into the challenges faced, the victories celebrated, and the paths carved by the pioneering individuals who gave birth to this vibrant field. With this foundation, readers can now delve deeper into research methodologies, exploring the diverse domains and applications of NLP. The remaining chapters will gradually introduce various concepts, algorithms, and techniques, serving to empower beginners in their quest to master the art of Natural Language Processing. The adventure begins-now.

1.3 Navigating the Terrain: Applications and Implications

As we delve deeper into the fascinating world of Natural Language Processing (NLP), it becomes essential to understand the vast range of applications and the profound implications it holds for various domains. NLP encompasses the utilization of artificial intelligence and linguistics to enable machines to understand, interpret, and process human language in a meaningful manner.

One area where NLP has made significant strides is in the field of information retrieval. With the exponential growth of digital data, the ability to extract relevant information from vast amounts of unstructured textual data has become a critical necessity. NLP algorithms can sift through mountains of text, categorize information, and provide timely access to relevant knowledge. This aids in a variety of applications such as search engines, sentiment analysis, and sentiment classification.

Furthermore, NLP is increasingly employed in the realm of text generation and language translation. Machine translation has progressed considerably from rule-based approaches to more sophisticated neural network architectures, allowing for more accurate and fluent translations between languages. In addition, automated content generation, like article writing or summarization, benefits from NLP techniques that enable machines to generate coherent human-like text.

In recent years, sentiment analysis has attracted considerable attention from both academia and industry. Sentiment analysis leverages NLP to determine the sentiment expressed in a piece of written or spoken text. This has profound implications for industries such as market research, customer relationship management, and social media analytics. Companies can now process customer feedback, gauge public opinion, and make data-driven decisions based on sentiment analysis results.

Beyond the realm of practical applications, NLP also influences social and ethical aspects of technology. As we strive to develop increasingly intelligent systems capable of processing human language, questions of privacy, bias, and fairness emerge. Ensuring that NLP algorithms respect users' privacy and do not perpetuate discriminatory practices is crucial. NLP researchers and practitioners need to constantly reflect on the societal impact of their work and diligently work towards creating ethical systems.

Another significant implication of NLP lies in its potential to bridge language barriers and enable cross-cultural communication. As humans, we are now more interconnected than ever, and NLP has a vital role to play in promoting understanding and breaking down barriers. Imagine a world where language is no longer a barrier to knowledge sharing, diplomacy, or commerce - NLP has the power to bring this closer to reality.

Moreover, NLP finds its application in the healthcare domain. Electronic health records, medical literature, and patient communication are immense sources of valuable information, but often locked away in unstructured text. NLP techniques facilitate efficient extraction and analysis of this data, enabling healthcare professionals to make data-driven decisions, improve patient outcomes, and advance medical research.

In conclusion, navigating the terrain of NLP entails exploring a vast landscape of applications and understanding the wide-ranging implications it holds. From information retrieval to language translation, sentiment analysis to ethical considerations, NLP has transformative potential across various domains. Harnessing the power of NLP can revolutionize industries, enhance global communication, and contribute to societal progress. As a beginner venturing into the realm of NLP, it becomes essential to research and embrace the rich possibilities in order to navigate this ever-evolving landscape.

1.4 Charting the Course: Roadmap to Mastery

Embarking on the journey of mastering Natural Language Processing (NLP) can feel like setting sail into uncharted waters. As a beginner, navigating through this vast field can be overwhelming, with its complex algorithms, deep learning models, and numerous application areas. However, with a well-designed roadmap and the right guiding compass, any aspiring NLP enthusiast can chart their course to mastery.

The art and science of NLP revolves around enabling computers to understand, interpret, and generate human language. With the explosion of textual data in today's digital age, NLP has become a crucial field with applications ranging from sentiment analysis and chatbots to machine translation and voice assistants. As an active research area in the field of artificial intelligence, NLP combines techniques from various disciplines such as linguistics, machine learning, and computer science to tackle the intricate challenges involved.

For beginners, the roadmap to mastering NLP starts with a strong foundation in programming and data manipulation. Proficiency in Python, a versatile and widely used language, is essential for NLP practitioners. Understanding basic concepts of object-oriented programming, data structures, and algorithms is a prerequisite before delving into the intricacies of NLP. Libraries like NLTK (Natural Language Toolkit) and spaCy provide powerful tools and resources that can aid beginners in their initial understanding and exploration of NLP techniques.

With a strong programming background in place, the next step on the journey is acquiring knowledge about the fundamental concepts of linguistics. Understanding the structural and semantic aspects of language is crucial for designing effective NLP models. Concepts such as syntax, morphology, and semantics lay the groundwork for extracting useful information from textual data and generating coherent responses. Studying linguistic theories and analyzing natural language corpora can provide valuable insights into the intricacies of human language, helping beginners develop a deeper understanding of NLP techniques.

Once well-versed in language fundamentals, it is time to delve into the core techniques of NLP. Familiarity with concepts like tokenization, part-of-speech tagging, named entity recognition, and sentiment analysis allows beginners to process and analyze textual data, which forms the bedrock of NLP applications. Implementing these techniques using specialized libraries and tools is crucial for gaining hands-on experience and becoming proficient in practical NLP tasks.

As beginners navigate through the initial stages of their NLP journey, the roadmap gradually leads them into the realm of advanced techniques such as machine learning and deep learning. Understanding the concepts behind algorithms like Support Vector Machines (SVM), Hidden Markov Models (HMM), and Recurrent Neural Networks (RNN) equips learners with powerful tools for language modeling, text classification, sequence labeling, and more. Leveraging libraries like scikit-learn and PyTorch, beginners can train and evaluate models using real-world datasets, honing their skills in applying machine learning techniques to NLP problems.

In addition to grasping the theoretical underpinnings of NLP, experimenting with state-of-the-art models and frameworks is also vital for mastery. Gaining expertise in frameworks like Transformers, BERT, GPT, and ELMO allows beginners to leverage pre-trained models on a variety of NLP tasks, achieving higher accuracy and efficiency. Staying updated with research papers, attending conferences, and participating in online NLP communities provide avenues for learning about the latest advancements and techniques in the field.

As beginners progress through their NLP roadmap, it is crucial to build a project portfolio by working on real-world, hands-on applications. By solving practical problems and participating in Kaggle competitions or similar platforms, aspiring NLP practitioners can showcase their skills, collaborate with experts, and build a network within the NLP community. This practical experience further refines their knowledge and prepares them for the challenges they may encounter in their future endeavors.

In conclusion, mastering Natural Language Processing is a journey that encompasses multiple disciplines and requires dedication, persistence, and continuous learning. By following the roadmap outlined above, beginners can navigate through the complexities of NLP, progressively honing their skills, and charting their course to becoming proficient NLP practitioners. As they embrace this ever-evolving field, they have the potential to contribute to groundbreaking innovations that transform the way we interact with computers and enhance our understanding of language in the digital age.

Chapter 2: The Linguistic Tapestry

2.1 The Melody of Phonetics: Harmony in Speech

In the intricate tapestry woven by language, speech is the thread that brings thoughts to life. It is a symphony of sounds, carefully orchestrated by the speaker, carrying with it not just the intended meaning, but also emotions, cultural subtleties, and interpersonal connections. This beautiful array of phonetic elements, known as phonemes, dances together to create the melody we hear when we listen to someone speaking.

Phonetics, the study of these speech sounds, is a fascinating field within linguistics that explores the intricacies of human vocal communication. It delves into the physical properties of sound production, the way sounds are organized and combined into words, and how different individuals pronounce the same sounds in distinctive ways.

Understanding phonetics is essential for everyone working in Natural Language Processing (NLP), a discipline that aims to bridge the gap between human language and computational systems. NLP is driven by the goal of enabling machines to understand, interpret, and generate fluent and meaningful human-like language. To achieve this feat, it is vital to grasp not only the structure and semantics of language but also the nuances of pronunciation and phonetic context that can greatly influence comprehension. The first step in unlocking the secrets of phonetics lies in differentiating between phonetic and phonemic representations. Phonetics is concerned with the physical properties of sounds themselves, such as their resonance, pitch, duration, and articulation, whereas phonemics focuses on the abstract mental representations and distinctions that sounds carry within a particular language system. This distinction is crucial because although two different phonetic sounds might sound similar to the human ear, they can have completely different phonemic meanings in a specific linguistic system.

The study of phonetics encompasses various subfields, including articulatory phonetics, acoustic phonetics, and auditory phonetics, each examining different aspects of sound production, transmission, and perception. Articulatory phonetics investigates how speech sounds are formed and articulated within the vocal tract, studying concepts such as place of articulation, manner of articulation, and voicing. Acoustic phonetics analyzes the physical properties of sound waves produced during speech, studying parameters like frequency, intensity, and duration. Auditory phonetics explores the perception and categorization of speech sounds by studying how the brain interprets and processes the auditory input it receives.

To navigate the multifaceted domain of phonetics, a solid foundation in phonetic transcription is essential. Phonetic transcription is a system that represents speech sounds using a set of symbols, such as the International Phonetic Alphabet (IPA). The IPA provides a unified representation of all human speech sounds, regardless of language or dialect, enabling linguists and NLP researchers to accurately and consistently capture the intricacies of pronunciation.

Through phonetic transcription, researchers can analyze the phonetic characteristics of speech, investigate cross-linguistic variations, and identify common patterns that emerge within and between languages. Such insights are invaluable not only for improving automatic speech recognition systems and text-to-speech synthesis but also for applications like accent recognition, pronunciation training, and language teaching tools.

As a beginner delving into the vast expanse of Natural Language Processing, comprehending the melody of phonetics and the art of transcription is a critical step. By understanding the nuances of speech sounds and how they are organized, one lays the foundation for building sophisticated language models that can truly bridge the gap between humans and machines, ensuring that our conversations and interactions with technology become more intuitive, natural, and harmonious.

2.2 Morphological Mosaics: Crafting Words from Roots

Language, as a tool for communication, possesses an intricate and fascinating structure. One of the most fundamental building blocks of language is the morpheme, the smallest meaningful unit within a word. Morphemes can be further classified into two main types: free morphemes, which can stand alone as words, and bound morphemes, which need to be attached to other morphemes to convey meaning.

In the realm of natural language processing (NLP), understanding morphemes and how they combine to form words is crucial. Just as a mosaic artist assembles small tiles to create a larger image, language utilizes a similar principle by combining morphemes to craft an array of words with diverse meanings. This exploration of word formation, known as morphology, sheds light on the structural patterns and rules that underpin language.

Morphological processes play a significant role in expanding our lexicon and ensuring the construction of new words from existing morphemes. By reshuffling, adding, or removing morphemes, language adapts and evolves to meet the ever-changing needs of its users. For beginners diving into the fascinating world of NLP, comprehending these patterns is vital for tasks such as word tokenization, lexical analysis, and beyond.

At the core of morphology lies the concept of affixes, which can either be prefixes (attached at the beginning of a word), suffixes (affixed at the end), or infixes (placed within the word). These morphological wonders allow for the creation of words by modifying a base or root morpheme. A root morpheme carries the central meaning of a word and remains unaffected by affixation.

Through the systematic application of affixes, the possibilities for word creation become endless. For instance, the prefix "un-" can be attached to words to express negation or reversal, completely changing the meaning. Take the word "happy." When we add the prefix "un-," it transforms into the opposing concept of "unhappy". A similar approach can be taken with bound morphemes such as suffixes. For example, adding the suffix "-ed" to "laugh" changes it to "laughed," indicating that the action happened in the past.

Apart from prefixes and suffixes, another crucial aspect of morphology involves the concept of roots and stems. These truncated units often carry the bulk of a word's meaning and serve as platforms for affixation. They can be fully functional words on their own or a simplified version of a word. Interestingly, different languages can assign different roles to the root and stem, which further adds to the intricacy and variety of linguistic systems.

For NLP beginners seeking to unravel the secret behind morphological mosaics, diving deep into the rich tapestry of language's constituent parts is essential. Understanding how individual morphemes operate, discerning the roles of affixes, roots, and stems, and studying the diverse processes that forge words through combining these building blocks will unlock the door to a whole new level of language comprehension.

As the journey into the depths of morphology unfolds, tools such as morphological analyzers and parsing algorithms become indispensible. These tools, based on extensive linguistic knowledge and paired with computational techniques, provide invaluable assistance in identifying, classifying, and gathering information about morphemes and their organization within words. With each step taken on this linguistic quest, the magic and complexity of language as a creative force unfold. Morphological mosaics lie at the very heart of linguistic expression and serve as fertile ground for the endeavors of natural language processing. By apprehending the rules governing the formation of words, beginners are better equipped to tackle the challenges and intricacies of meaningful language analysis in the realm of NLP, leading to enhanced machine understanding and human-like interactions.

2.3 Syntax Symphony: The Grammar Orchestra

As we dive further into our exploration of Natural Language Processing, we come across the fascinating realm of syntax, a critical aspect of language understanding. Among this chapter, we will embark on a melodic journey through the intricacies of syntax, unveiling the Symphony of the Grammar Orchestra.

Just as an orchestra blends multiple musical instruments to create harmonious notes, so does the grammar orchestra harmonize the elements of language to convey meaning. Grammar, the underlying structure and arrangement of words and phrases, plays a pivotal role in the construction of sentences, enabling us to communicate effectively.

To comprehend the birth of syntax, it is imperative to understand its foundation: the relationship between words. A sentence, as we know, consists of individual words and their connection to one another. Syntax explores the rules governing how these words should be sequenced to produce well-formed and meaningful sentences.

Imagine a symphony orchestra preparing for a performance. Each musician, equipped with their musical instrument, has a specific role, diligently following the conductor's instructions. Similarly, in the grammar orchestra, each word corresponds to a linguistic unit with a particular function, precisely positioned within a sentence under syntactic rules.

Let's meet the musicians of our Grammar Orchestra. First, we have the noun section, representing people, places, or things. They form the backbone of a sentence, portraying the main actors or objects of interest. Then, the verb section enters, working in perfect sync with the nouns, expressing the action, occurrence, or state of being. Adjectives, adept at enhancing and complementing nouns, bring vibrant colors to our melodic sentences.

Next, the adverb section joins the orchestra, guiding and modifying verbs, imparting nuances of time, manner, place, or frequency to the action being performed. In the background, the preposition section subtly dictates the relationship between nouns and other elements within a sentence, whether it's about direction, time, or location.

Ah, let us not forget the conjunction section, forging connections between words, phrases, or clauses, enabling seamless transitions and conjoint expression. Coordinating conjunctions enhance teamwork, joining similar elements, while subordinating conjunctions gracefully elucidate dependencies between phrases or clauses.

But hold your applause; we cannot overlook the mighty interjections. Often injecting emotions, surprises, or exclamations, interjections provoke resonance within the Grammar Orchestra's performance, adding a touch of spontaneity and humanism.

As the Grammar Orchestra takes the stage within the field of Natural Language Processing, researchers strive to uncover its underlying rules and principles. Pioneers delve deep into linguistic theory, intricately analyzing sentences and developing formal frameworks to discern the composition and structure of grammatically sound utterances.

This research in syntax not only aids in language understanding but also forms a fundamental basis for various NLP applications like sentence parsing, machine translation, and more. The examination of syntax empowers NLP models to grasp the syntactic structure of sentences, thus generating coherent and contextually accurate responses.

Quiver your curiosity and delve into the world of syntax, where the Grammar Orchestra harmonizes the arrangement of words to produce meaningful expression. By exploring the rules and conventions of language structure, we venture closer to unraveling the mysteries of human communication, equipping us with the tools to unlock the true potential of Natural Language Processing.

2.4 Semantic Splendor: Exploring Meaning in Language

Amidst the vast expanse of language lies a realm of intricacies that continues to captivate linguists, computer scientists, and language enthusiasts alike - the fascinating world of semantics. Within this intricate domain, the study of meaning in language, Natural Language Processing (NLP) ventures to unravel the inherent complexity of linguistic expression and comprehend the intricacies of semantic splendor.

Semantic analysis, a foundational aspect of NLP, seeks to decipher the meaning embedded within words, phrases, and sentences. Researchers grapple with diverse challenges as they endeavor to enable machines to truly understand human language at a deeper semantic level. Deciphering the intricacies of language meaning is no simple feat, equipped only with a basic lexicon and syntactic framework. For machines to comprehend language as humans do, they need to delve into intricate nuances and establish connections not only between words but also the ideas and concepts they represent. This journey involves exploring the monumental interplay between words and their meanings, relationships, and contextual associations.

At its core, semantic analysis aims to enable machines to accurately interpret the rich tapestry woven by human communication. This includes navigating the treacherous use of polysemous words that possess multiple meanings based on context. Resolving ambiguity represents a formidable challenge, as it necessitates understanding syntax, encompassing references, and discerning between literal and figurative language.

A fundamental approach to semantic analysis involves utilizing word embeddings - dense vector representations of words that embody their meaning in a multidimensional space. By training models on vast amounts of textual data, machines acquire an intrinsic understanding of word semantics and their relationships with their surrounding linguistic context. These word vectors enable researchers to capture semantic similarities and disparities, facilitating tasks such as word categorization, word sense disambiguation, and concept clustering.

As raw text undergoes semantic analysis, machines endeavor to map it onto a conceptual graph, creating a semantic representation. This graph captures the essence of meaning in a finite, comprehensible form. Rich with relationships between words, concepts, and entities, this graph is a testament to the vast landscape of semantic knowledge, encapsulating not just single dimensions of meaning but interconnected webs of thought and interpretation. Through extensive parsing, pattern recognition, and machine learning techniques, machines identify recurrent semantic patterns, allowing them to detect intricate sentiments, identify subjectivities, and uncover sentiment-modifying factors within a given document.

Nevertheless, despite significant progress, semantic analysis stubbornly retains its elusive nature. The depth of human linguistics and the dynamism of contextual interpretations continues to challenge even the most advanced NLP systems. As new words emerge, and long-standing semantic paradigms evolve, harnessing the entirety of meaning in a language remains an exercise in constant evolution and adaptation.

Accompanied by the rapid advancement of machine learning techniques, the pursuit of semantic splendor in NLP continues unabated. Researchers tirelessly experiment with sophisticated algorithms, explore ever-growing language corpora, and investigate lexical and syntactic features to improve semantic interpretation. They strive to empower machines to embrace language nuances, metaphorical expressions, and abstract concepts, thus propelling NLP systems closer toward true understanding of human thought and communication.

Within this vast and ever-expanding landscape of semantics, the quest to decipher meaning remains an exhilarating pursuit - one that invites both seasoned linguists and curious beginners to embark on a profound exploration of linguistic richness. As NLP technologies unfold their wings beyond the realm of semantics, the understanding of language and the subsequent possibilities enter an expanse that promises to deliver new arenas of innovation, comprehension, and marvel through the intimate interfusion of machines and human expression.

2.5 Pragmatic Pathways: Understanding Context

In the quest to unravel the complexities of Natural Language Processing (NLP), researchers often find themselves navigating through the intricate web of context. Context acts as the backbone of language comprehension, providing the necessary backdrop against which utterances and text can be analyzed for meaning. Housed within this chapter, we delve into the fascinating world of context and its essential role in NLP.

Context refers to the set of circumstances, both environmental and linguistic, that shape the meaning of words, phrases, and sentences. Humans naturally leverage the power of context to effectively communicate and comprehend language. For example, consider the sentence, "I saw a beautiful bird outside." The word "bird" on its own does not provide much information, but when viewed in the context of the word "beautiful" and the location being "outside," it greatly narrows down the possible interpretations.

Understanding context is crucial in NLP applications, as it allows us to bridge the gap between written or spoken words and their intended semantics. However, context is not a straightforward concept to grasp, as it encompasses various layers and forms that require deep analysis. Let's explore some of the key facets of context in NLP.

One essential aspect of context is co-reference resolution. In language, many words or expressions refer to other entities or events mentioned earlier or later in text or conversation. Resolving these references accurately is vital for understanding the intended references correctly. Consider the sentence, "John saw a dog. It was chasing a cat." The word "it" refers to the dog mentioned earlier. Co-reference resolution techniques aim to identify and link such references, allowing the text to be comprehended seamlessly.

Another crucial aspect of context is understanding the temporal dimension. Language is inherently bound by time, and grasping the temporal context is fundamental for proper interpretation. Consider the sentence, "The sun sets at 6 pm." The meaning of "sets" greatly depends on its temporal context, as it signifies a specific action tied to the evening hours. NLP systems incorporate temporal analysis to account for time-related references, thereby capturing the right essence of utterances.

Furthermore, pragmatic context plays a vital role in determining implied meanings and pragmatic interpretations. Pragmatics explores how language is used in different contexts to fulfill specific goals beyond the mere exchange of information. Pragmatic context allows NLP models to decipher metaphors, sarcasm, politeness, and other nuanced linguistic phenomena. For instance, in the sentence, "Can you please pass the salt?," the pragmatic interpretation revolves around the speaker's polite request rather than a literal analysis of words. Incorporating these pragmatic dimensions is critical for accurate understanding of language in context.

Cultural and situational context should also be taken into account in NLP research. Different cultures and situations influence language usage, idiomatic expressions, and social norms. Understanding these contextual elements is essential for building NLP systems that can adapt to diverse user contexts and provide culturally relevant and sensitive outputs.

As researchers dig deeper into contextual analysis, a wide range of techniques and approaches emerges. These include rule-based systems, machine learning, statistical models, and deep learning architectures. Each approach leverages different strategies to capture and exploit contextual information effectively.

The study of context in NLP is an ongoing pursuit toward imbuing AI systems with a true understanding of language. By delving into various forms of context, such as co-reference, temporal dimensions, pragmatic inferences, cultural and situational factors, and by employing various computational techniques, researchers can continually refine NLP models to comprehend language in a more nuanced and sophisticated manner.

Basic knowledge and research understanding of these different facets of context will provide you with a solid foundation in tackling the inherent challenges of Natural Language Processing. To better comprehend the dynamic nature of language, we now move ahead to exploring the intricacies of sentiment analysis in the next section.

Chapter 3: Textual Alchemy: Preprocessing

3.1 Tokenization: Breaking the Linguistic Seal

As you embark on your journey to delve into the field of Natural Language Processing (NLP), you will soon realize the importance of tokenization, the initial step that unveils the hidden structure within textual data. Speaking of structures, have you ever contemplated the essence of linguistic expressions as they form the bridges connecting words, phrases, and sentences? Just like breaking a seal, tokenization allows us to unravel the intricate tapestry woven by language.

Tokenization, defined as the process of segmenting text into fragments referred to as tokens, serves as a cornerstone of NLP, opening the door to a myriad of applications and algorithms within this fascinating domain. By breaking down textual data into smaller chunks, tokenization sparks a series of subsequent analyses, exploration, and interpretation, enabling computers to comprehend and maneuver the complexities of human language.

Tokens, in this case, can be seen as the indivisible units of language, representing distinct entities such as words, punctuation marks, or even subwords if desired. To gain a comprehensive understanding, it's crucial to recognize that tokenization varies according to the granularity we seek. Fine-grained tokenization aims to split the text into smaller units, encompassing not just words but also capturing morphological variations, linguistic nuances, and intricacies of written language, such as contractions or hyphenated compounds. On the other hand, coarse-grained tokenization focuses on classes or larger-scale units, such as sentences or paragraphs, producing a holistic view of the text.

However, the process of tokenization is not as straightforward as it may first appear. After all, language is brimming with challenges, be it ambiguous phrases, idiomatic expressions, or multilingual utterances. Relying solely on the delimiters between words or sentences becomes insufficient and error-prone when identifying tokens, especially when dealing with informal or non-standard language. Furthermore, distinguishing between tokens and their roles becomes a nuanced task when blended expressions emerge, incorporating multiple words or elements, coined names, abbreviations, or numerical values.

To address these challenges, NLP practitioners employ a wide range of techniques, tools, and algorithms. These approaches incorporate mathematical and statistical models, rule-based methods, or a hybrid combination, employing AI-powered models such as deep learning and neural networks. Techniques such as sentence tokenization, word tokenization, and subword tokenization each play an integral role in breaking down the linguistic seal in different language processing scenarios.

Despite the advances in tokenization algorithms, iterative efforts persist in refining techniques to cater to the diverse range of complexities and transformations that language imposes. Researchers continuously strive to adapt tokenization methods to suit specific domains, including medical literature, legal documents, and social media data, molding their application to fit evolving linguistic landscapes effectively.

As a beginner in the realm of NLP, embracing tokenization not only provides myriad opportunities but also sets the stage to dive deeper into higher-level language analysis, information extraction, and sentiment analysis. Just like archaeologists carefully examine, categorize, and understand the fragments they uncover, successful tokenization opens the gates to exploration and deeper semantic understanding within textual data.

So, as you sharpen your skills and discover the wonders of language processing, remember the power hidden within tokenization, as it breaks the linguistic seal, paving the way for natural language understanding, information retrieval, and a realm of possibilities. With each token revealed, new insights await and NLP will perpetually propel us towards a future where human-computer interaction seamlessly engulfs us in a world of comprehension and linguistical marvels.

3.2 Clearing the Canvas: Filtering Noise with Stopword Magic

As the journey into the realm of Natural Language Processing (NLP) for beginners continues, we now arrive at the third section of our tutorial - "Clearing the Canvas: Filtering Noise with Stopword Magic". Buckle up, as we delve deeper into the fascinating and crucial step of preprocessing text data to eliminate unnecessary noise.

Imagine yourself as an artist embarking on a creative endeavor. You have a beautiful canvas ready to be painted upon, but before you can start, you must clear away the clutter cluttering your workspace. In NLP, text data serves as our canvas, and employing stopword magic helps us remove the unnecessary clutter or noise that obstructs our understanding of the actual content.

So, what exactly are stopwords? Stopwords are commonly used words that do not add much meaning to a text. Examples include words such as "the," "and," "to," and "is." While these words are essential for constructing grammatically correct sentences, they often provide little helpful information when it comes to understanding the overall context.

Filtering out stopwords from our text data serves multiple purposes. First, it aids in reducing computational complexity. By eliminating words that contribute little significance, we can concentrate our computing resources on more important tasks. Secondly, removing stopwords improves the quality of our downstream NLP tasks, such as text classification or sentiment analysis, as it allows the focus on the keywords and phrases that hold substantial meaning. Lastly, it aids in shrinking the size of our data, making it easier to work with and potentially enhancing the overall performance and efficiency of our algorithms. Now that we understand the importance of removing stopwords, let's explore some common techniques used in NLP to achieve this. One of the simplest approaches is to create a predefined list of stopwords and filter them out from our text data. These lists contain words that are commonly found in natural language, but have little semantic importance. However, it's important to note that the composition of these stopwords lists may vary depending on the requirements of your specific NLP task or language particularities.

In addition to predefined lists, another technique employed is the use of statistical methods to identify and remove stopwords. Here, the frequency distribution of words is used to differentiate between stopwords and significant terms. Words that appear frequently across documents but have limited value in representing the core content are flagged as potential stopwords.

To implement these techniques, various NLP libraries provide built-in functionalities. For instance, the popular library NLTK (Natural Language Toolkit) in Python offers a comprehensive stopwords module that supports multiple languages. Simply by importing this module, you gain access to a consolidated set of stopwords.

However, it is important to exercise caution because each problem domain and dataset can have its own specific requirements. Sometimes, using generic stopwords lists might hinder the performance of the system or overlook domain-specific terms that are crucial for analysis. In such cases, it becomes imperative to generate or augment the default stopwords lists to cater to the unique characteristics of the data at hand.

As our exploration of NLP continues, be prepared to discover and harness more advanced techniques that aid in efficient noise filtering and data transformation. In the next section, we will dive into the fascinating process of stemming and lemmatization, where we aim to further enhance the accuracy and coherence of our text data. So stay curious, for there are many more exciting facets of NLP awaiting our exploration.

3.3 Stemming and Lemmatization: The Art of Word Transformation

3.3 Stemming and Lemmatization

As our journey in the field of Natural Language Processing (NLP) continues, we delve deeper into the world of word transformation. Words are the building blocks of any language, and in order to analyze and process textual data effectively, we need to understand the different forms that words can take. This understanding is critical for tasks such as information retrieval, text classification, sentiment analysis, and machine translation, among others.

Within this section, we explore two powerful techniques that aid in word transformation: stemming and lemmatization. Both techniques focus on reducing words to their root form, but they approach the task using different strategies. Let us dive into the details of these methods and their applications in NLP.

3.3.1 Stemming

Stemming is a process of reducing words to their base or root form by removing affixes or inflections. The resulting form, known as the stem, may not always be a valid word in the language but represents the core semantic meaning of the original word. Stemmers use heuristic algorithms and word structure rules to perform this transformation.

Let's consider an example to understand the concept better. Suppose we have a dataset of movie reviews, and we want to analyze the sentiment of the reviewers. By applying stemming, we can group together words with the same root, which helps in reducing the vocabulary size and avoids duplications. For instance, the words "running," "runs," and "runner" would all be reduced to the common stem "run." This collapse of similar words facilitates analysis while allowing us to retain the essential meaning behind each word.

Stemming algorithms are language-specific and consider linguistic characteristics. Some well-known stemming algorithms include the Porter stemming algorithm, the Snowball stemming algorithm (also known as the Porter2 algorithm), and the Lancaster stemming algorithm. These algorithms have their own strengths and weaknesses, which make them suitable for particular language or task requirements.

Despite its usefulness, stemming has limitations. Since it is based on rules and patterns, it can occasionally generate incorrect stems or fail to produce the desired result for certain words. For example, it may incorrectly stem the word "connection" as "connect" instead of its semantic root, "connects." Nevertheless, stemming remains a widely used technique in many NLP applications due to its simplicity and efficiency.

3.3.2 Lemmatization

Unlike stemming, lemmatization aims to transform words to their meaningful base form, known as the lemma. This not only reduces words to their root but also ensures their validity in the language. The lemmatization process takes into account the morphological analysis of words and applies a lexical knowledge base, such as a dictionary or a thesaurus, to achieve accurate results.

Consider the word "better" as an example. Stemming would yield "better," which is already a valid word, but lemmatization would transform it to its lemma, "good." The lemmatizer recognizes the underlying meaning of the word and provides a more interpretable representation.

Lemmatization, albeit more accurate than stemming, is computationally more expensive and slower due to its reliance on more complex linguistic algorithms. It takes into account the part of speech (POS) of a word before finding its lemma. For example, "saw" would be correctly lemmatized to "see" instead of a nonsensical word like "saw."

Moreover, lemmas can provide valuable information for tasks such as text generation and language understanding. They allow for the identification of concepts and relationships between words within a sentence or document. Lemmatization plays a vital role in various NLP applications, including information retrieval, question answering systems, and dialogue generation.

In conclusion, stemming and lemmatization are crucial techniques in the field of Natural Language Processing. While stemming focuses on reducing words to their core form, lemmatization goes a step further to derive their meaningful base form. Stemming is efficient but may occasionally generate incorrect stems, whereas lemmatization provides accurate results at the cost of increased complexity. Understanding the art of word transformation through stemming and lemmatization equips us to explore the vast possibilities and challenges of NLP further.

3.4 Parts of Speech: The Grammar Palette

As we delve deeper into the fascinating field of Natural Language Processing (NLP), it becomes crucial for beginners to understand the building blocks of language. One essential aspect of language analysis is the identification and categorization of the different parts of speech – the words that make up sentences.

When we communicate, we instinctively use a variety of words – some denote objects, while others describe actions or express emotions. Recognizing and classifying these words into their respective categories is done using a framework called the Grammar Palette. Just as an artist uses a palette to mix and match colors to create an artwork, the Grammar Palette helps NLP algorithms identify and understand the structure and meaning of sentences.

The Grammar Palette consists of multiple parts of speech, each serving a unique purpose in a sentence. Let's take a closer look at the main parts of speech:

1. Nouns: Nouns are used to identify people, places, things, or concepts. They form the backbone of any sentence, providing the subjects and objects necessary for understanding. Nouns can range from tangible objects like "car" or "tree" to abstract ideas such as "love" or "freedom."

2. Pronouns: Pronouns are a category of words that serve as replacements for nouns. Instead of using the same noun repeatedly, pronouns save us from redundancy. Common pronouns include "he," "she," "it," "they," and "we." They allow us to swiftly refer back to previously mentioned people, places, or things.

3. Verbs: Verbs are dynamic words that express actions or states of being. They bring life to sentences, illustrating what a subject is doing or experiencing. Examples of verbs include "run," "eat," "sleep," and "think." Verbs are the core elements that animate sentences and convey movement and change.

4. Adjectives: Adjectives add vivid descriptions and details to nouns, enhancing their meaning. They help paint a clearer picture by expressing qualities, characteristics, or attributes. Adjectives encompass words like "beautiful,"

"strong," "happy," and "tall." They allow us to create more compelling and specific descriptions within sentences.

5. Adverbs: Adverbs modify verbs, adjectives, and other adverbs, enabling us to express manner, time, frequency, degree, or place. They provide more precision and context to actions and descriptions. Adverbs often end in "ly," such as "quickly," "happily," "intensely," and "everywhere."

6. Prepositions: Prepositions show the relationships between different nouns, pronouns, or other parts of speech in a sentence. Common prepositions include "in," "on," "at," "under," and "over." They help us understand where something is in relation to something else. Prepositions are the glue that connects different elements of a sentence together.

7. Conjunctions: Conjunctions join words, phrases, or clauses, creating cohesiveness and flow within sentences. They enable us to combine thoughts and link different ideas. Examples of conjunctions include "and," "but," "or," and "because." Without conjunctions, sentences would appear disjointed and lack logical progression.

8. Determiners: Determiners precede and modify nouns, helping specify or generalize their meaning. They introduce and define the scope of nouns in particular contexts. Words like "the," "a," "this," and "many" fall under the category of determiners. They indicate whether we are referencing specific or unspecific items.

By recognizing and comprehending these foundational parts of speech, beginning NLP researchers can unravel the intricate details of a sentence's structure. Natual Language Processing algorithms can utilize this knowledge to associate meaning to words, facilitate language translation, interpret sentiment analysis, and much more.

As we continue our exploration into the depths of NLP, understanding the Grammar Palette unlocks a plethora of opportunities for language comprehension, driving us closer to developing AI systems capable of emulating human communication. So, let's grab our virtual Grammar Palette and embark on this exciting journey of language analysis and manipulation!

3.5 Entity Extraction: Unveiling Linguistic Gems

In the world of Natural Language Processing (NLP), the task of entity extraction holds great importance. It involves identifying and categorizing specific entities within a given text such as names, dates, locations, organizations, and more. This intricate process helps computers understand the structure and meaning behind human language and is a fundamental step towards achieving true NLP capabilities.

Entity extraction plays a crucial role in numerous applications, ranging from information retrieval and sentiment analysis to question answering systems and machine translation. By identifying and extracting relevant entities, NLP systems can provide more accurate and personalized responses, aiding in automating various aspects of information processing.

The process of entity extraction can be challenging due to the ambiguity of language, wherein words may have multiple meanings or refer to different entities depending on the context. For instance, the word "apple" could represent a fruit, a multinational technology company, or even an idiom. Therefore, developing effective techniques for entity extraction requires a combination of linguistic knowledge, statistical models, and innovative algorithms.

One widely adopted approach to entity extraction involves exploiting linguistic features and patterns. By analyzing the syntactic structure of the text, identifying named entities, and understanding their relationships within the given context, NLP systems can extract valuable information. For example, consider the following sentence: "John visited Paris last month." An entity extraction system would recognize "John" as a person and "Paris" as a location, thus gaining insights about the actions and connections between them.

To enhance the accuracy and effectiveness of entity extraction, researchers have leveraged machine learning algorithms. By training models on large annotated datasets, these algorithms can learn to recognize various entity types and their corresponding contextual clues. This process of supervised learning empowers NLP systems to generalize from training data and effectively handle unseen entities in real-world scenarios.

Another major area of research in entity extraction is focused on tackling the challenge of domain-specific entity recognition. While many existing models perform well in general contexts, they may struggle when applied to specialized fields like medicine, finance, or law. To address this, researchers have explored domain adaptation techniques that transfer knowledge from general domains to specific ones, improving performance on targeted applications.

Furthermore, to truly unveil the linguistic gems embedded in text, entity extraction systems need to handle real-world complexities. These complexities include misspellings, abbreviations, colloquial language, and various forms of user-generated content. Researchers have been working diligently to develop algorithms that can mitigate these challenges, allowing NLP systems to extract and recognize entities accurately and reliably across a wide range of text sources. Entity extraction has evolved considerably over the years, moving from rule-based systems to data-driven techniques and neural architectures. This progression has paved the way for significant advancements in various domains, including information retrieval, healthcare analytics, and social media analysis. As research continues, the extraction of linguistic gems from vast pools of textual data is expected to play a pivotal role in building more intelligent and robust NLP systems.

Chapter 4: Mapping Meaning: Text Representation

4.1 The Patchwork Quilt: Building with Bag-of-Words

In the vast realm of Natural Language Processing (NLP), one prominent technique that has revolutionized text analysis and understanding is the Bag-of-Words (BoW) model. Imagine a patchwork quilt, where every square in the quilt represents a distinct word from a corpus of text. These squares are then stitched together to form a comprehensive representation of the document or a collection of documents. Similar to how a quilt binds patches to create a cohesive and visually intriguing pattern, the BoW model combines individual words to capture information and uncover insights.

For beginners delving into the field of NLP, understanding the foundations of the BoW model is essential. At its core, BoW involves transforming raw text data into a format that facilitates analysis and machine learning algorithms. This approach disregards the sequential order and grammatical structure of words, instead emphasizing the frequency of occurrence within a document. By constructing a "bag" of words, we can represent a document or a collection of documents as a numerical vector, enabling computational algorithms to process and make sense of textual information.

To build a BoW model, several steps are involved. The initial stage requires compiling a corpus, a collection of texts used for analysis. This corpus can be as small as a single document or as extensive as a massive dataset spanning diverse sources. Once the corpus is defined, it undergoes a process called tokenization. Tokenization involves breaking down texts into individual entities, typically words or phrases called tokens. Each token serves as a patch in our quilt, encompassing the central elements of our document.

Next, we perform data preprocessing, which helps eliminate noise and irrelevant information while refining the corpus. This step includes removing punctuation, numbers, and stop words - commonly occurring words that tend to offer little semantic value, such as "the" or "and". Additionally, stemming or lemmatization may be employed to reduce tokens to their base or root form, enabling even more effective analysis. These preprocessing techniques meticulously design the quilt squares, refining them before our model is stitched together.

As the pieces come together, an integral step initiates: constructing a feature matrix. This matrix quantifies the presence or absence of words across all documents, allowing us to weave useful insights. Each row corresponds to a specific document, while each column denotes a unique word from our tokenized corpus. The cells contain the frequency, weight, or even binary indication of word occurrence. With this constructed matrix, striking patterns begin to emerge, patterns that were initially concealed among the vast texts forming our corpus.

However, the BoW model has distinct limitations. By ignoring the order and structure of words, it fails to capture the contextual nuances present within language. Furthermore, nuances implicit within word placement or syntactic structure are often overlooked. Although BoW fractures information regarding word arrangement, it successfully enables a broad range of applications, including document categorization, sentiment analysis, and information retrieval.

As beginners explore the patchwork world of NLP and the BoW model, one vital aspect is to recognize its multitude of applications. From uncovering insights hidden within social media networks to enabling language translation systems, NLP with BoW empowers machines to delve deeper into language-based analytics. By harnessing the patchwork approach, NLP enthusiasts can build systems that understand, interpret, and process human language efficiently - one stitch at a time.

4.2 TF-IDF: Weighing Words' Worth

In the vast realm of Natural Language Processing (NLP), a highly regarded technique used to analyze and understand textual data is the TF-IDF (Term Frequency-Inverse Document Frequency) model. This method plays a pivotal role in determining the significance of words within a document by assigning a weight that reflects both their frequency within the document and their occurrence across the entire corpus. The importance of incorporating TF-IDF into NLP research lies in its ability to extract meaningful insights from large volumes of text.

TF-IDF operates on the principle of assessing the relevance of a word by examining two main metrics: term frequency and inverse document frequency. Term frequency measures the frequency of a given word within a document. It highlights the importance of a term by simply counting the number of occurrences, implicitly implying a notion of significance based on regular appearances.

However, a challenge lies in dealing with noisy words that appear repeatedly in different documents without contributing substantial information, such as prepositions or articles. In order to address this issue, inverse document frequency is employed to provide further insight into the overall importance of a term. It calculates the negative logarithm of the fraction of documents in which a specific term appears. This measure penalizes widely occurring words and helps bring focus to words that are more unique and descriptive of the context.

The TF-IDF score is then computed by multiplying the respective term frequency with inverse document frequency values. The resulting score is thus a float that represents the relative importance of a word within a document compared to its occurrence throughout the entire corpus. By assigning such weights, researchers in NLP can uncover key insights, identify significant themes or topics, and even detect patterns or anomalies within large collections of text.

The TF-IDF model provides a nuanced approach for weighing the worth of words in a document, emphasizing their relative importance and discounting those that are frequent in everyday language. This technique finds applications in various NLP tasks, such as document classification, information retrieval, text summarization, and even sentiment analysis. By recognizing and assigning greater importance to words that appear less frequently yet offer more meaningful content, the TF-IDF method empowers NLP researchers to delve deeper into textual data and extract valuable knowledge efficiently.

To put TF-IDF into practice, one must first preprocess the data by applying techniques such as tokenization, stemming, and stop-word removal. These steps help break down the text into individual words or terms, remove redundant variations, and eliminate commonly used words that have little bearing on the overall meaning.

Beyond basic understanding, it is essential to consider certain additional factors when utilizing the TF-IDF model. One crucial aspect is corpus size; larger collections of documents generally provide more accurate and robust TF-IDF scores. Additionally, researchers should be wary of text that is highly domain-focused, as it may call for customization of the TF-IDF model to ensure its applicability within a specific context.

In conclusion, TF-IDF represents a fundamental technique that serves as a building block for numerous NLP applications. By leveraging the assessment of term frequency and inverse document frequency, this method empowers researchers to weigh words' worth within a document or larger corpus accurately. It uncovers meaningful insights from large amounts of text, facilitating the extraction of valuable knowledge and aiding in understanding the meanings and nuances behind textual data. As aspiring NLP practitioners, researching and harnessing the potential of the TF-IDF model will undoubtedly prove to be an essential step towards mastering the intricacies of Natural Language Processing.

4.3 Word Embeddings: Painting Pictures with Words

As we dive further into the vast realm of natural language processing (NLP), an intriguing and pivotal concept emerges – word embeddings. Just like an artist's brushstrokes can convey depth and beauty to a canvas, word embeddings have become a fundamental tool in capturing nuanced meanings and relationships within language.

To understand word embeddings, we must first grasp the notion of how computers perceive textual data. Traditionally, computers view words as isolated entities, oblivious to any semantic or contextual connotations they may possess. However, language is inherently dynamic and complex, often relying on the context in which words appear to fully comprehend their intended meanings. This is where word embeddings come in.

Word embeddings offer a way to represent words in vector space, taking into account not only their lexical qualities but also the surrounding linguistic context. By assigning each word a vector representation such that semantically similar words have closer vector distances, word embeddings allow computers to capture intricate intricacies like synonymy, contextual relevancy, and even degrees of similarity between words. In other words, rather than looking at words individually, word embeddings provide a holistic perspective that enables machines to capture the essence of language more organically.

The beauty of word embeddings lies not only in their ability to embody semantic nuances but also in the variety of techniques one can employ to generate them. Among the most popular methods is the widely acclaimed Word2Vec, a tool invented by Tomas Mikolov et al. at Google in 2013. Word2Vec is trained on massive amounts of text corpora and achieves word representations by predicting surrounding words given a target word or vice versa. This process infuses the vectors with semantic understanding, creating embeddings that encapsulate contextual similarities.

Another notable approach is GloVe (Global Vectors for Word Representation), developed by Jeffrey Pennington et al. at Stanford University in 2014. Unlike Word2Vec, GloVe leverages co-occurrence statistics to generate word embeddings. By examining how frequently words appear together in a corpus and contrasting this with their independent probabilities, GloVe brings forth embeddings that capture not only syntactic but also semantic relationships.

Regardless of the method used, word embeddings have proved invaluable in a plethora of NLP applications. From machine translation and sentiment analysis to question-answering systems and even recommendation engines, word embeddings empower machines to grasp the subtleties of human language and perform more human-like tasks. Perhaps one of their most remarkable applications is in fraud detection, where anomalies in word embeddings can expose potentially fraudulent behavior more effectively than traditional methods.

However, as with any powerful tool, word embeddings are not without limitations. One major challenge lies in the notion of polysemy – words with multiple meanings. For instance, the word "bank" can refer to a financial institution or the edge of a river. While humans easily disambiguate such words using their surrounding context, word embeddings struggle to capture the various contexts and typically generate a single vector representation that encompasses all possible meanings.

Moreover, training word embeddings requires significant computational resources and extensive data. Building large-scale models that genuinely capture the richness of language can prove both time-consuming and computationally intensive. Consequently, researchers continue to explore methods for generating high-quality word embeddings using less resource-intense approaches.

In conclusion, word embeddings defy the traditional notion of words as isolated units, unveiling the capacity of machines to comprehend language more deeply. By considering the surrounding context and capturing nuanced associations, word embeddings enable computers to paint pictures with words, unraveling intricate semantic connections that were once elusive. As we delve further into this fascinating field of NLP, the power of word embeddings becomes increasingly evident, paving the way for more advanced language processing and understanding.

4.4 Document Embeddings: Portraits of Textual Context

As we venture further into the realm of Natural Language Processing (NLP), one of the crucial aspects that emerges is the need to comprehend the contextual nuances inherent within textual data. Fortunately, advancements in machine learning techniques have paved the way for the development of document embeddings, which serve as intricate portraits, capturing the essence and depth of textual context, enabling computers to derive valuable insights from reams of written information.

What makes document embeddings revolutionize NLP is their ability to encapsulate the semantic relationships and latent meaning present within a piece of text, regardless of its length. No longer do we have to rely solely on bag-of-words or sequential models, as document embeddings empower us to understand the intricate interconnectedness between words, sentences, and paragraphs, also uncovering the implicit semantics hidden therein.

At its core, the creation of document embeddings relies on the principle of vector representation. By transforming words and sentences into dense numerical vectors, document embeddings make it possible to quantify and compare textual context—an endeavor that has been historically challenging for computers. Imagine encoding the entirety of War and Peace into vector portraits! This enables us to navigate the vast landscape of text-based records with relative ease, paving the way for efficient search algorithms, automated summarization, sentiment analysis, and even question-answering systems.

There exist numerous techniques for generating document embeddings. One prominent family of methods is based on the concept of word embeddings. Word2Vec, GloVe, and FastText are among the most widely used word embedding models that have significantly contributed to further developments in document embeddings. By leveraging these models' learnings, we can aggregate and craft larger vectors that represent entire documents, capturing the nuances and semantic information, unlocking valuable insights typically hidden within the conventional textual format.

Depending on the specific requirements and objectives, different algorithms can be employed for the generation of document embeddings. One popular approach is the average of word embeddings, where individual word vectors are summed over their respective dimensions and averaged, giving rise to a representation of the document as a "mean" of its constituent words. This approach finds its usefulness in scenarios where general meaning or sentiment of a document suffices for the task at hand.

For more fine-grained representations, algorithms such as Paragraph Vectors (like Doc2Vec) came to the forefront. These models extend the ideas of word embeddings by incorporating document-level information. While performing training, they jointly learn to encode both words and documents into vectors that ensure similarity between related texts and dissimilarity between unrelated ones, creating a dynamic and contextually aware embedding space.

Convolutional Neural Networks (CNN) and Recurrent Neural Networks (RNN) have also shown remarkable success in generating document embeddings. CNNs can capture local patterns by utilizing filters of varying sizes to convolve over the document, enabling the network to capture meaningful n-gram representations. RNNs, on the other hand, leveraging their sequential nature of processing text, excel in preserving context by iteratively updating the document embedding based on subsequent events—an especially useful characteristic for tasks such as sentiment analysis or narrative understanding.

With document embeddings in our NLP repertoire, fascinating applications begin to unfold. Imagine a system that can effortlessly identify similar documents from millions of records, facilitating rapid knowledge extraction and mining. Or an algorithm that, when fed the corpus of all scientific literature, could retrieve relevant research papers based on a query containing keywords and phrases. Augmented by these representation techniques, document embeddings become invaluable tools, empowering us to delve deeper than ever before into the vast expanses of textual data.

Continuing recent efforts in advancing NLP research, document embeddings provision us with unparalleled means to investigate, analyze, and comprehend textual information allowing governments, researchers and businesses to tap into the untapped potential. As we navigate this exciting field, we begin to unravel the untold stories nestled within textual expressions—stories that have long been a challenge for machines to comprehend. With document embeddings, we embark on a transformative journey, enabling computers to truly understand the complex tapestry of words, traversing deeper into the texts woven by the minds of authors, poets, and scholars throughout time.

Chapter 5: Crafting Language Models

5.1 N-grams: Tracing Patterns in the Linguistic Labyrinth

As we venture further into the intricacies of Natural Language Processing (NLP), we come across a precious tool that allows us to unlock hidden patterns within the linguistic labyrinth: N-grams. In the enchanting world of NLP, N-grams act as guides, relentlessly tracing the footprints of language and unraveling its mysteries.

N-grams are a powerful concept used to construct and model the structure of texts. They are essential for various NLP tasks such as language modeling, speech recognition, and machine translation. N-grams, simply put, are contiguous sequences of words or characters that act as building blocks for linguistic analysis. The "N" in N-grams represents the number of words or characters contained within each sequence. Tri-grams, for example, consist of three words, while bi-grams consist of two.

Armed with these N-grams, we embark on a thrilling journey through the corners of text, picking up cues and patterns along the way. Let us imagine that we have a sentence: "The quick brown fox jumps over the lazy dog." If we break this sentence down into bi-grams, we would end up with: ["The quick", "quick brown", "brown fox", "fox jumps", "jumps over", "over the", "the lazy", "lazy dog"].

By analyzing the frequencies of these bi-grams, we can gain insights into how words are connected and co-occur in text. This understanding allows us to build models that capture the essence of language, capturing its fluidity and capturing the soul of words.

However, N-grams do not stop at bi-grams or tri-grams; they can extend further. We can have four-grams, five-grams, or even n-grams, where "n" represents any arbitrary number. The choice of the N-gram order depends on the problem at hand; a higher order presents a more detailed perspective on language, but also increases the computational complexity.

To perform meaningful analysis, we also need a representative corpus of text to source our N-grams. This corpus can range from books to articles, tweets to legislative documents, each containing a vital piece of the linguistic jigsaw puzzle. By feeding these documents into our N-gram model, we commence a sort of detective work, uncovering recurring phrases, idiomatic expressions, common collocations, or even the building blocks of syntactic structures.

Gaining access to an extensive corpus offers an indispensable resource for study and research, augmenting our understanding of language nuances and idiosyncrasies. With the advent of digital libraries, vast web repositories, and powerful search engines, a treasure-trove of readily available information and text awaits exploration, ready to be transformed into valuable insights through the magic of N-grams.

As we refine our N-gram models, various challenges arise, such as handling out-of-vocabulary words or adjusting to the particularities of different languages. Researchers meticulously delve into these challenges, embarking on a journey of discovery that pushes the boundaries of NLP.

So take a deep breath, summon your courage, and join us as we venture further into the realm of N-grams, gracefully tracing patterns in the enigmatic linguistic labyrinth. Equipped with curiosity, determination, and the tools of NLP, we become explorers on a quest to deepen our comprehension of human language and bring it closer to machines – as if seeping a touch of life into our digital creations.

5.2 Neural Networks: The Symphony of Synapses

As our journey into the realm of Natural Language Processing continues, we now delve into the magnificent world of neural networks. Often hailed as the symphony of synapses, neural networks bring us closer to unlocking the true potential of machine learning in processing human language.

Before we immerse ourselves in the intricate workings of neural networks, let us understand why they hold such tremendous promise. Human brains, marvels of evolution, are intricately wired networks of neurons that allow us to think, process, learn, and communicate. Taking inspiration from our own cognitive systems, scientists and researchers devised artificial neural networks, attempting to replicate the complex workings of the human brain within the confines of computer algorithms and software.

At a fundamental level, a neural network is composed of interconnected nodes called neurons. These neurons are arranged in layers, forming what is known as an artificial neural network. While simplistic, this metaphorical representation is surprisingly effective in mimicking the computation performed by the brain. The first layer in a neural network is the input layer, where data is ingested and processed. Each node in this layer corresponds to a specific attribute or feature of the input. For instance, in natural language processing, these nodes may represent words, characters, or grammatical structures present in a text.

Moving forward, we encounter hidden layers within the neural network. These hidden layers play a crucial role in information processing, as they transform the input data into a higher-level representation. Through the process of forward propagation, the information propagates from one layer to the next, with each hidden layer carrying out a specific computation using the input data. This process of gradually processing the information results in the extraction of higher-level features and patterns.

The final layer in the neural network is the output layer. As the name suggests, it generates the output based on the computations performed in the hidden layers. In the context of natural language processing, this output may correspond to a sentiment classification (positive, negative, neutral) or even a language translation.

But how does a neural network learn from the input data to generate the desired output? This is where the concept of training comes into play. During the training process, the neural network goes through a series of iterations, adjusting the strength of the connections between the neurons to minimize the difference between the predicted output and the actual output. This adjustment is carried out by optimizing a mathematical function called a loss function, which quantifies the difference between the predicted and desired outputs.

One popular method of training neural networks is called backpropagation. This technique involves traversing the network backward, from the output layer to the input layer, and adjusting the weights of the connections between neurons based on the calculated loss. This iterative process of tweaking the weights gradually refines the network until it becomes more accurate in generating the desired output.

Now equipped with a foundational understanding of neural networks, we can start exploring their applications within the realm of natural language processing. These include sentiment analysis, text classification, machine translation, named entity recognition, and many more. Neural networks have proven to be adept at extracting insights from unstructured text data, enabling us to analyze, understand, and extract valuable information from large volumes of text.

As we venture further into the world of artificial intelligence, it becomes evident that neural networks, the symphony of synapses, hold incredible potential in revolutionizing how we process language. Harnessing the power of these computationally inspired algorithms, we can further unlock the mysteries of human communication and pave the way for intelligent machines capable of comprehending and responding to our language with astonishing accuracy. Moreover, the continuous advancement of neural networks and their applications will undoubtedly shape the future of Natural Language

Processing, presenting endless opportunities for both researchers and practitioners alike.

5.3 Transformers: Shaping Linguistic Futures

It is impossible to discuss the field of Natural Language Processing (NLP) without addressing the revolutionary impact of transformers. In recent years, transformers have emerged as a game-changer in shaping the linguistic future of this rapidly advancing field. This chapter delves into the concept of transformers, their role in NLP, and their transformative potential.

In the early days of NLP, traditional techniques heavily relied on intricate combinations of algorithms, heuristics, and handcrafted features to handle various linguistic tasks. These approaches were often limited by the lack of scalability, flexibility, and generalization capabilities. However, the development of transformers revolutionized NLP by introducing a fundamentally new and powerful paradigm for language representation.

The key idea behind transformers lies in their attention mechanism. Instead of relying solely on sequential processing, transformers enable models to consider the dependencies among all words in a sentence simultaneously. This parallel processing capability not only allows for more effective and efficient language understanding but also captures long-range dependencies that were difficult to model previously. It was this breakthrough that opened the door to significant advancements in a wide range of NLP tasks, including language translation, sentiment analysis, question answering, and text generation.

One of the most influential transformer models in NLP is the Bidirectional Encoder Representations from Transformers (BERT) model. BERT, introduced by Devlin et al. in 2018, fundamentally changed the landscape of pre-training techniques for language understanding tasks. Instead of solely relying on supervised training, BERT introduced the concept of unsupervised pre-training followed by fine-tuning on specific downstream tasks. By pre-training deep bidirectional representations on an extensive corpus, BERT achieved state-of-the-art performance on multiple benchmark datasets, showcasing the transformative power of transformers in NLP.

Building upon the success of BERT, subsequent models such as GPT (Generative Pretrained Transformer) and T5 (Text-To-Text Transfer Transformer) further elevated the capabilities of transformers. GPT showcased the potential of transformers in generating coherent and contextually relevant text, taking language generation to new heights. T5, on the other hand, introduced a unified framework that transformed various NLP tasks into a text-to-text format, demonstrating the versatility and efficiency of transformer-based architectures.

The wide-ranging successes of transformers in NLP have not only transformed the research landscape but have also shaped the future of practical applications. Various cutting-edge language models based on transformers, such as OpenAI's GPT-3, have gained immense attention due to their remarkable abilities to generate realistic and context-aware language. These models have paved the way for advancements in conversational AI, chatbots, virtual assistants, and even creative writing, opening up unprecedented possibilities.

It is important to mention that there are still challenges and limitations to be addressed in the realm of transformers. Issues such as model size, training data biases, interpretation of learned representations, and computational resource requirements continue to pose obstacles. However, ongoing research and technological advancements suggest that the linguistic future shaped by transformers holds immense potential.

In conclusion, transformers have taken the field of NLP by storm, leading to significant advances and shaping the linguistic future. With their ability to capture long-range dependencies and process information in parallel, transformers have transformed traditional NLP approaches and opened up new possibilities. Their impact is evident in state-of-the-art models such as BERT, GPT, and T5, as well as in practical applications like language generation and conversational AI. While challenges persist, transformers represent a pivotal milestone in the evolution of NLP, propelling researchers and practitioners towards the next frontier of linguistic understanding and technology.

5.4 Evaluating Linguistic Artistry: Metrics and Measures

When it comes to Natural Language Processing (NLP), the focus is not only on understanding the syntax and semantics of human language but also on evaluating the artistic quality of the output generated by NLP systems. Evaluating the linguistic artistry of NLP is crucial to determine how effectively these systems can mirror human-like language generation.

Linguistic artistry evaluates the aesthetics, creativity, and effectiveness of human language use. Traditional NLP metrics typically focus on objective measures such as accuracy, precision, and recall, which are essential for tasks like machine translation and sentiment analysis. However, assessing the linguistic artistry of NLP output requires a more nuanced approach.

In recent years, researchers have sought to develop metrics and measures to evaluate the linguistic artistry of NLP systems. This involves considering factors such as word choice, fluency, coherence, and the overall naturalness of the generated text. These metrics aim to capture the quality of language outputs with finer-grained analysis, moving beyond accuracy-based evaluations.

One widely-used metric for evaluating linguistic artistry is BLEU (Bilingual Evaluation Understudy). BLEU calculates the similarity between machine-generated text and human-generated reference text, providing a score that represents the quality of the generated text. However, BLEU has limitations–– it primarily focuses on surface-level word overlaps rather than capturing nuances in overall language quality.

To address the limitations of BLEU, other metrics like METEOR (Metric for Evaluation of Translation with Explicit ORdering) and ROUGE (Recall-Oriented Understudy for Gisting Evaluation) have been proposed. METEOR measures both surface-level word overlaps and semantic similarity, providing a more comprehensive evaluation of language quality. ROUGE, on the other hand, focuses on evaluating text summaries and represents another aspect of linguistic artistry.

Additionally, researchers have explored measuring fluency and coherence in NLP output. Perplexity, a metric borrowed from language modeling, has been used to assess the fluency and coherence of generated sentences. Lower perplexity scores indicate more coherent and natural-sounding text. Other metrics, such as grammaticality and understandability, are being considered to capture specific aspects of linguistic artistry.

The challenge in evaluating linguistic artistry lies in developing metrics that correlate well with human perception of language quality. Subjective evaluation methods, such as human judgments and crowd-sourced assessments, play a crucial role in complementing automated metrics. Analyzing user feedback and conducting user studies are essential for validating the proposed metrics and improving their reliability.

While progress has been made in developing metrics to evaluate linguistic artistry in NLP, this field of research is still evolving due to the inherent complexity of language and the subjective perception of quality. Continuing efforts to enhance metrics and measures, as well as incorporating user feedback, will help improve the evaluation of linguistic artistry in NLP systems.

In conclusion, evaluating the linguistic artistry of NLP output goes beyond traditional NLP metrics. It requires considering factors such as word choice, fluency, coherence, and overall naturalness of the generated text. Metrics like BLEU, METEOR, and ROUGE attempt to capture linguistic artistry, while measures like perplexity, grammaticality, and understandability provide further insight. Additionally, incorporating subjective evaluation methods is vital to ensure metrics align with the human perception of language quality. Improving the evaluation of linguistic artistry in NLP will continue to be a challenging but important pursuit as we strive for more human-like language generation.

Chapter 6: Classifying Textual Realms

6.1 Supervised Learning: Guided Voyages in Classification

Part 6.1: Supervised Learning - Guided Voyages in Classification
In the vast field of Natural Language Processing (NLP), one of the fundamental aspects that beginners must grasp is supervised learning. This technique is often referred to as guided voyages in classification, as it allows machines to learn from labeled training data and then apply that learning to classify new, unseen data.

Supervised learning revolutionized the realm of NLP, providing a systematic framework to tackle complex language-based tasks. Classification, a key component of supervised learning, involves categorizing text or documents into predefined classes or categories. By training models on labeled datasets, these systems become capable of automatically assigning appropriate labels to new inputs.

The process of supervised learning begins with data collection and annotation. Developers gather a diverse set of text data that represents different classes or categories they want the model to learn. For instance, in sentiment analysis, one might collect positive and negative sentiment-labeled texts for training. These curated datasets serve as a reference point for the model to build its classification abilities.

Once the labeled dataset is ready, various machine learning algorithms can be employed to train models specifically designed for classification tasks. One of the most commonly used algorithms is Naive Bayes, which leverages probabilistic principles to classify new instances based on patterns found in the training data. Alongside Naive Bayes, algorithms such as decision trees, support vector machines (SVM), logistic regression, and neural networks are also widely applied in NLP classification tasks.

To accomplish successful classification, features, or attributes, of the text are extracted during the preprocessing phase. This involves transforming the raw input—such as sentences, paragraphs, or entire documents—into a computationally manageable format. Common techniques involved include tokenization, stemming, removing stop words, and converting text into numerical representations. These transformed features are utilized as inputs to training algorithms.

With the training phase complete, the resulting model is then evaluated using a separate labeled dataset known as the test set. The evaluation metrics account for how accurately the model can categorize unlabeled instances according to the designated classes. Successful models achieve high precision, recall, and F1 scores, indicating their ability to correctly predict class labels.

One of the primary challenges in supervised learning for NLP lies in ensuring the training dataset's quality and representativeness. Biases, incorrect labeling, or imbalances across classes can severely hamper the model's generalizability and performance. Rigorous data exploration and labeling techniques are crucial to building reliable classification models that exhibit broader applicability to real-world scenarios.

Furthermore, supervised learning excels in scenarios where the classifications to be performed are well-defined and the features are distinguishable within the input. It may face limitations when encountering highly nuanced or ambiguous situations, where human intuition and contextual understanding play a vital role. This limitation paves the way for more advanced techniques like unsupervised learning and deep learning, which seek to address these complexities.

Supervised learning has revolutionized the way we approach NLP tasks, enabling systems to adapt and classify text data at an unprecedented scale. Its potential applications are vast, ranging from sentiment analysis, document classification, spam detection, and question answering, to name just a few. Researchers and developers continue to push the boundaries of supervised learning to unlock deeper insights from textual data and enhance the performance of NLP models.

As beginners delve into the fascinating world of NLP, understanding supervised learning becomes paramount. Mastering the techniques and algorithms involved in guided voyages of classification opens up endless possibilities in language processing, allowing individuals to develop intelligent systems capable of comprehending and analyzing text in ways previously unimaginable. The journey into supervised learning is an essential step towards unraveling the true potential of Natural Language Processing.

6.2 Unsupervised Learning: Exploring the Unknown

In the vast field of Natural Language Processing (NLP), one of the most intriguing yet challenging areas is unsupervised learning. It is the realm of exploring the unknown, where the data holds no predefined labels or categories. Instead, the goal is to uncover patterns, relationships, and structures within the data itself. This chapter delves deep into the world of unsupervised learning, equipping beginners with the necessary tools to embark on this exciting journey.

Unsupervised learning is particularly fascinating because it allows us to unlock hidden insights and discover unknown knowledge from unstructured data. By removing the limitations of labeled data, it provides a powerful approach for analyzing language without any prior assumptions. This is particularly valuable in scenarios where data is vast and heterogeneous, such as social media, scientific articles, or even large corpora of books.

The first step to harnessing the potential of unsupervised learning is data preprocessing. Embedded within this initial stage, various techniques are applied to clean the data, remove noise, and transform it into a suitable format for further analysis. This may involve tokenization, where the text is split into meaningful units such as words or sentences, or normalizing the data to ensure consistency in language patterns.

Once the data has been preprocessed, the next challenge in unsupervised learning is feature extraction. Embedded within this phase, the goal is to retain the most relevant and significant information from the data while discarding irrelevant or redundant elements. Common approaches include techniques like Bag of Words (BoW), where the frequencies of words are used as features, or TF-IDF (Term Frequency-Inverse Document Frequency), which measures the importance of a term in a document relative to the entire corpus.

With the preprocessed and feature-extracted data in hand, unsupervised learning algorithms come into play. One of the most popular methods is clustering, which aims to group similar data points together based on their characteristics. Using algorithms like k-means or hierarchical clustering, the data is analyzed to identify clusters or groups that share common patterns or themes. This enables researchers to uncover latent structures or even discover new topics within the data.

Another powerful approach is dimensionality reduction, which aims to reduce the complexity of the data while maintaining its important features. Techniques like Principal Component Analysis (PCA) or t-SNE (t-Distributed Stochastic Neighbor Embedding) can be employed to transform high-dimensional data into lower dimensions, making it easier to visualize or comprehend.

Unsupervised learning also includes techniques like anomaly detection, which focuses on identifying abnormal or unusual data points that deviate from expected patterns. This is particularly valuable in detecting fraud or identifying outliers in a dataset, where the rare occurrences may hold significant insights.

One of the greatest challenges in unsupervised learning is evaluating the performance and quality of the results obtained. Since there are no predefined labels or metrics for comparison, it becomes a subjective assessment. Researchers rely on measures such as silhouette coefficient, homogeneity, or purity to evaluate the effectiveness of clustering algorithms and fine-tune the parameters to enhance the results.

Overall, unsupervised learning allows us to dive into the depths of unexplored data, unleashing its hidden knowledge and untapped potential. It empowers researchers and organizations to extract meaningful insights from large and complex datasets without relying on predefined labels or prior assumptions. As beginners embark on their journey through the realm of unsupervised learning in the field of Natural Language Processing, the challenges and rewards are sure to captivate their curiosity and drive them to push the boundaries of knowledge discovery.

6.3 Performance Metrics: Gauging Classifier Prowess

As we delve deeper into the realm of Natural Language Processing (NLP), it becomes imperative to evaluate the performance of classifiers. Learning about the various metrics used to measure the efficacy of these classifiers becomes crucial as we strive to fine-tune our models and achieve ever-higher levels of accuracy.

Performance metrics serve as yardsticks for gauging the prowess of classifiers. Inside this section, we will explore some of the common and widely-used performance metrics that go hand-in-hand with NLP. By investigating these metrics, we can gain a nuanced understanding of the performance capabilities of our classifiers.

One of the most basic metrics is accuracy - the measure of how often the classifier correctly predicts the class label. It is calculated by dividing the number of correct predictions by the total number of instances. Although accuracy provides a general overview of classifier performance, it is not always sufficient on its own. We must consider other metrics to uncover a more comprehensive picture.

Precision and recall are two significant metrics for evaluating classifier performance. Precision emphasizes the proportion of positive predictions that are accurate, taking into account false positives. On the other hand, recall measures the proportion of actual positives correctly identified by the classifier. Researchers and practitioners often strive for a balanced combination of precision and recall, striking a delicate trade-off to achieve optimal results.

F1 score, or the F-measure, conveniently combines both precision and recall into a single metric. This metric considers the harmonic mean of the two scores, reflecting a clustering of classifier prediction accuracy and its ability to correctly identify target classes.

Another performance metric gaining popularity is the Receiver Operating Characteristic (ROC) curve, accompanied by the Area under the Curve (AUC) metric. These metrics relate class separability and the trade-off between True Positive Rate (TPR) and False Positive Rate (FPR). By comparing different classifiers using the ROC curve, we can visually discern the classifiers' discrimination abilities and determine which model performs better.

Furthermore, in NLP, it is crucial to consider metrics specifically adapted to deal with imbalanced data. For instance, when dealing with sentiment analysis, the data may have an abundance of one sentiment (e.g., positive) and a scarcity of other sentiments (e.g., negative or neutral). In these cases, metrics such as macro-averaged and micro-averaged precision and recall should be employed to provide a more accurate representation of classifier performance.

In addition to the above-mentioned metrics, it is important to measure the execution time of classifiers, especially for large-scale NLP tasks involving vast amounts of data. Understanding the trade-offs between accuracy and execution time is vital, as it not only impacts computational efficiency but also provides insights into how well a given model can scale.

As aspiring practitioners in the field of NLP, it is paramount to grasp the significance of these performance metrics. By comprehensively evaluating the classifiers and delving into the nuances of their abilities, we can refine our models to achieve top-notch results. Only through continued research, experimentation, and dedication to understanding these metrics, can we unlock the true potential of Natural Language Processing.

6.4 Real-world Chronicles: Applications and Case Studies

Amid this section, we delve into the fascinating realm of real-world applications and case studies that demonstrate the power and potential of Natural Language Processing (NLP). These unique chronicles highlight the diverse range of industries in which NLP is being successfully employed, revolutionizing the way we interact with technology and transforming many aspects of our daily lives.

One compelling application of NLP can be found in the field of healthcare. Medical professionals are using NLP techniques to extract valuable insights from vast amounts of patient records, research papers, and clinical notes. By analyzing this unstructured data through text mining and information extraction, NLP algorithms can detect patterns, aid in diagnosis, predict disease progression, and even identify potential drug interactions. These groundbreaking advances not only enhance patient care but also contribute to more efficient healthcare systems worldwide.

Another exciting application lies within the realm of customer service and support. Many companies have deployed virtual assistants, commonly known as chatbots, which utilize NLP technologies to understand and respond to customer queries in real-time. These chatbots can interpret customer messages, extract relevant information, and provide tailored solutions and recommendations. By leveraging NLP, businesses can streamline their customer support processes, reduce response times, and ensure consistent and personalized assistance around the clock.

NLP is also transforming the world of finance and investment. Financial institutions are now employing powerful algorithms to analyze vast quantities of news articles, financial documents, and social media sentiment in real-time. By applying NLP techniques such as sentiment analysis and information extraction, these algorithms can infer the impact of news events on stock prices, predict market trends, and generate valuable insights for traders and investors. This integration of NLP into financial analysis enhances decision making, reduces risks, and facilitates autonomous trading systems.

Legal sectors are also discovering the immense potentials of NLP. Law firms and legal professionals are increasingly relying on NLP tools to automate time-consuming tasks, such as contract analysis, due diligence, and legal research. By employing techniques like natural language understanding and machine learning, NLP systems can extract relevant information from legal documents, summarize case laws, and generate legal recommendations. These advancements enable legal practitioners to improve their efficiency, reduce costs, and access reliable information at an unprecedented rate.

Additionally, NLP plays a significant role in the domain of social media and online platforms. Analyzing the huge volumes of text data generated on social platforms, NLP enables brands to understand customer sentiments, opinions, and preferences. This insight is invaluable for businesses in developing marketing strategies, improving brand reputation, and augmenting customer engagement. Whether it's analyzing Twitter feeds, Facebook comments, or customer reviews, NLP provides businesses with a comprehensive understanding of the ever-evolving landscape of consumer perception.

As we delve deeper into these real-world applications and case studies, it becomes evident that NLP is shaping the way we interact with technology and unlocking immense possibilities. From transforming healthcare to revolutionizing customer service, enhancing financial analysis to automating legal processes, NLP is a powerful tool that touches various aspects of our lives. As technology continues to advance, we can expect NLP to push the boundaries further, opening up new avenues for exploration and innovation.

Chapter 7: Deciphering Sequences

7.1 Named Entity Recognition: The Quest for Linguistic Treasures

In the ever-evolving field of Natural Language Processing (NLP), a valuable and fascinating treasure beckons linguists and computer scientists alike: named entities. These linguistic treasures encompass any real-world entities such as people, organizations, locations, date expressions, monetary values, and more. Extracting and understanding this valuable information from text documents, social media posts, and other textual data is the quest sought by researchers in the domain of Named Entity Recognition (NER).

Named Entity Recognition involves the identification and classification of named entities within text, tracing its roots back to the early days of computational linguistics and gaining momentum with the advancements in machine learning and NLP algorithms. This specific task of NLP plays a critical role in numerous downstream applications, such as information retrieval, question answering systems, text summarization, machine translation, and sentiment analysis, to name just a few.

The primary goal of Named Entity Recognition is twofold: firstly, to identify mentions or instances of named entities within a given text; and secondly, to classify these mentions into predefined categories, such as person names, organization names, geographical locations, and so on. This two-step process makes NER a multi-label classification problem that requires sophisticated algorithms and knowledge resources.

To train models for Named Entity Recognition, datasets with annotated named entities are essential. These datasets serve as the foundation that enables the model to learn the patterns and characteristics of different named entities. The annotations in these datasets typically involve marking the start and end positions of each named entity within a given text, combined with the specific entity category it belongs to.

However, creating such annotated datasets is a labor-intensive task that demands linguistic expertise and considerable effort. Consequently, researchers have constructed numerous manually annotated corpora over the years to facilitate the development and evaluation of NER systems. Some well-known examples of these corpora include the CoNLL 2003 dataset, which encompasses news articles and presents four named entity categories (person, organization, location, and miscellaneous); the OntoNotes corpus that provides a larger and more diverse set of annotations, covering multiple domains; and the Wikigold corpus, which focuses on Wikipedia articles with entities like person, organization, and place names.

With the availability of such datasets, numerous strategies have been developed to address the Named Entity Recognition problem. Traditional rule-based approaches utilize handcrafted patterns, predefined gazetteers, and linguistic knowledge to recognize named entities. These rule-based systems are often efficient and perform well when dealing with specific domains or tightly controlled environments.

On the other hand, statistical and machine learning techniques have paved the way for the development of data-driven approaches that rely on training models with annotated data. These models range from Hidden Markov Models (HMMs) and Conditional Random Fields (CRFs) to more recent advances utilizing deep learning architectures, such as Recurrent Neural Networks (RNNs), Convolutional Neural Networks (CNNs), and transformers. These data-driven approaches demonstrate impressive performance when it comes to named entity recognition on a wide range of texts with varying characteristics and domains.

NER systems also heavily rely on the availability and utilization of linguistic resources, such as part-of-speech taggers, syntactic parsers, and dictionaries. Leveraging these resources aids in disambiguating named entities, determining their boundaries, and providing additional contextual information, thus enhancing the accuracy of the recognition process.

However, the quest for linguistic treasures does not end with mere extraction and classification. Named Entity Recognition has further challenges tied to entity mentions within large-scale documents, cross-document identification, handling ambiguous references, and resolving aliases and coreferences. These challenges necessitate the integration of NER with other NLP tasks, like coreference resolution and semantic role labeling, to paint a more comprehensive picture of the named entities mentioned across vast texts.

As Named Entity Recognition continues to advance and refine its algorithms, NLP researchers and practitioners continually strive to enrich data, apply sophisticated machine learning techniques, and incorporate domain-specific knowledge resources to achieve remarkable results. Breakthroughs in this domain have paved the way for comprehensive information extraction, aiding in a variety of applications throughout the realm of Natural Language Processing. The quest for linguistic treasures continues, drawing expert linguists and computer scientists alike to unearth the invaluable named entities hidden within text, unlocking new realms of knowledge and understanding.

7.2 Part-of-Speech Tagging: Grammatical Guardians

I. This process involves identifying and categorizing each word in a text according to its grammatical role and context within a sentence. Part-of-speech (POS) tags can provide valuable insights into the syntactic structure and semantic meaning of a given textual input. Understanding the grammatical guardians behind part-of-speech tagging is imperative for beginners delving into the field of NLP.

II. The Significance of Part-of-Speech Tagging

Part-of-speech tagging serves as the gateway to a wide range of NLP applications, including machine translation, sentiment analysis, information retrieval, named entity recognition, and many others. By associating words with appropriate POS tags, NLP systems can glean insights about word-sense disambiguation, co-reference resolution, and overall understanding of sentence structure. Therefore, accurate POS tagging is integral to the success of NLP models and applications.

III. The Concept of POS Tags

Before diving deeper, it is essential to grasp the basic concept of POS tags. Each word in a sentence possesses a specific role, such as noun, verb, adjective, pronoun, adverb, or conjunction. POS tags act as linguistic labels that assign specific categories to words based on their syntactic function. For instance, in the sentence "The cat jumps over the fence," the word "cat" would receive the POS tag "noun," while "jumps" would be tagged as a "verb. "

IV. Approaches to Part-of-Speech Tagging

Various algorithms and techniques have been developed over the years to tackle the part-of-speech tagging challenge. These range from rule-based approaches to statistical modeling and machine learning methods. Rule-based approaches employ a set of predefined rules and linguistic patterns to assign POS tags to words. However, these approaches can be influenced by language-specific idiosyncrasies and might not generalize well across different languages.

Statistical modeling techniques utilize probabilistic methods, leveraging contextual information to assign POS tags. Hidden Markov Models (HMMs) and Conditional Random Fields (CRFs) are commonly used algorithms within this framework. These models rely on the observed words and their surrounding words to make informed predictions of POS tags, considering the context and potential co-occurrences.

More recently, deep learning approaches have gained attention, revolutionizing part-of-speech tagging. Techniques like Recurrent Neural Networks (RNNs) and Long Short-Term Memory (LSTM) networks have proven effective in capturing long-range dependencies and contextual information, making them popular choices for POS tagging tasks.

V. Challenges in Part-of-Speech Tagging

Part-of-speech tagging presents certain challenges due to language ambiguity, word sense variations, and viral linguistic structures. Homonyms, multi-word expressions, idiomatic phrases, slang, and evolving language trends create difficulties in accurately assigning POS tags. As a result, domain-specific adaptations, robust algorithms, and large-scale training data are necessary to overcome these challenges. Moreover, tagsets can vary across languages and grammatical systems, requiring NLP practitioners to adapt their models accordingly.

VI. Tools and Resources for Part-of-Speech Tagging

A plethora of tools and resources are available to assist beginners in part-of-speech tagging. Popular NLP libraries like NLTK, SpaCy, and Stanford CoreNLP offer comprehensive APIs and pre-trained models for POS tagging. These resources greatly simplify the process for beginners, allowing them to focus on building applications that leverage accurate POS tagging.

In addition to ready-made tools, building custom training datasets and fine-tuning models on specific domains can enhance POS tagging results. Annotated corpora like the Penn Treebank, Universal Dependencies, and Brown Corpus provide valuable training data for POS taggers.

VII. Conclusion

Part-of-speech tagging is a fundamental component of natural language processing, providing crucial information about word types and their syntactic roles within sentences. Understanding the various approaches, challenges, and tools available for POS tagging empowers beginners entering the field of NLP. With the ability to harness the grammatical guardians of language, NLP practitioners can unlock the potential of this powerful technology and create impactful applications across numerous domains.

7.3 Chunking: Breaking Textual Boulders

As we delve further into the realm of Natural Language Processing (NLP), we stumble upon an important concept that aids in deciphering the structure of text - chunking. This technique acts as a textual jackhammer, tearing through the intricately woven sentences, breaking them down into manageable chunks of information for further analysis. By identifying and grouping together phrases or words that share a common syntactic role, chunking paves the way for a more thorough understanding of the language.

Chunks, in the context of NLP, refer to defined phrases that are formed by combining consecutive words or tokens. These chunks serve as the building blocks for constructing more meaningful representations of textual data. Often, chunks consist of one or several words, but the specific rules governing their construction vary depending on the desired outcome.

One commonly used method for chunking is known as noun phrase chunking. Amidst this approach, the focus is on extracting chunks that encompass noun phrases in the text. These noun phrases typically consist of a noun and all its associated modifiers, such as adjectives or determiners. By grouping these elements together, we can discern valuable information about the objects, entities, or concepts present in the text.

To perform noun phrase chunking, various techniques and algorithms can be employed. One approach involves using part-of-speech tagging to assign a tag to each word in a sentence, indicating its grammatical function. By analyzing the resulting tags, we can identify patterns and rules that guide the formation of noun phrases. These patterns can be encoded using regular expressions or specialized grammars to facilitate the chunking process.

In addition to the noun phrase approach, there are other types of chunking that focus on different syntactic elements. For instance, verb phrase chunking seeks to extract meaningful phrases that involve verbs and their associated components. Similarly, prepositional phrase chunking identifies chunks that involve a preposition and the words that follow it.

The utility of chunking extends beyond mere syntactic analysis. It serves as a crucial step in more advanced NLP tasks, such as named entity recognition and information extraction. By isolating relevant chunks, we can better identify and extract valuable information from texts, enabling applications such as automatic summarization, question-answering systems, or sentiment analysis.

Furthermore, the accuracy of chunking heavily relies on the quality of the underlying linguistic resources and models. Proficient possession of accurate part-of-speech taggers, grammars, and knowledge about language structures is essential for effective chunking. Therefore, understanding the principles and nuances of chunking empowers NLP practitioners to craft robust and reliable systems.

As we conclude this exploration of chunking, we appreciate its function as a powerful tool within the NLP toolkit. Just as a skilled sculptor carefully chips away at a rock to reveal the hidden masterpiece within, chunking uncovers the latent semantic insights waiting to be harnessed within written text. Mastering this skill is a significant stepping stone towards understanding and effectively processing natural language while counting only tokenized words as they provide the bricks for constructing meaningful analyses and unlocking the true context of textual boulders.

7.4 Parsing Dependencies: Navigating Linguistic Webs

As we delve deeper into the world of Natural Language Processing (NLP), we come across an important concept known as parsing dependencies. It is through parsing dependencies that we can effectively navigate the intricate linguistic webs that form the backbone of human language.

When we communicate, we often convey our thoughts and ideas through a series of interconnected words that rely on specific syntactic relationships. Parsing dependencies allow us to identify and analyze these relationships, providing us with a deeper understanding of sentence structure, word roles, and overall meaning.

The process of parsing dependencies involves breaking down a sentence into its individual words and identifying the grammatical relationships between them. This can be a complex task, as linguistic webs can quickly become tangled with various levels of dependency.

One popular method for parsing dependencies is through the use of dependency graphs. These visual representations map out the relationships between words in a sentence, allowing us to see how they connect and interact with each other. By analyzing these graphs, we can extract valuable information such as subject-verb relationships, noun phrases, prepositional phrases, and much more.

To navigate these linguistic webs, significant research efforts have been put forth to develop algorithms and machine learning models specifically designed for parsing dependencies. These models analyze large corpora of already parsed sentences to develop rules and patterns for identifying and interpreting linguistic dependencies effectively.

Traditional parsing algorithms leverage manually created rules and heuristics to identify dependencies and construct the parse trees. However, more recent approaches have embraced the power of machine learning, using data-driven techniques to automatically learn the rules of dependency parsing.

One popular framework in dependency parsing is the arc-eager system, which navigates the linguistic webs by using a specific set of actions based on the topological characteristics of a sentence. It assigns roles to words such as "shift," "reduce," "left-arc," and "right-arc" to navigate through the parsing process.

Deep learning models, such as recurrent neural networks (RNNs) and transformer-based models like BERT, have also made significant advances in parsing dependencies. These models utilize neural networks to automatically learn and generalize the complex relationships between words, improving the accuracy and efficiency of dependency parsing.

The practical application of parsing dependencies spans across various NLP tasks. Sentiment analysis, question answering, machine translation, and information retrieval are just a few examples. By understanding the syntactic structure of a sentence, we can better analyze and extract meaning from text, enabling machines to interpret and respond to human language more intelligently.

As beginners in NLP, the daunting task of parsing dependencies might seem overwhelming. However, thanks to the advancements in research and the availability of robust tools and libraries, grasping this concept is more accessible than ever. By effortlessly integrating these tools into our projects, we can effectively harness the power of parsing dependencies to unlock a wealth of information hidden within the linguistic webs of human language.

Chapter 8: Sentiment Analysis: Unraveling Emotional Threads

8.1 Traditional Approaches: Gauging Emotional Undercurrents

Over the past few decades, natural language processing (NLP) has emerged as a field at the intersection of linguistics, computer science, and artificial intelligence. It aims to analyze and understand human language through computational techniques, empowering machines to process, interpret, and respond to textual data. NLP has found applications in various domains, including machine translation, sentiment analysis, information retrieval, and speech recognition, among others.

One specific area of interest within NLP is the understanding and detection of emotional undercurrents in texts. The ability to decipher emotions, such as happiness, sadness, anger, or fear, can greatly enhance human-computer interactions and open up new avenues for personalized experiences, targeted communication, and sentiment-aware applications. Traditional approaches to gauging emotional undercurrents in text have laid the foundation for further advancements in the field.

Traditional approaches in NLP primarily involved the use of rule-based systems and manual feature engineering. One commonly used method to analyze emotional content is sentiment analysis. Sentiment analysis, also known as opinion mining, is the task of determining the sentiment expressed in a given piece of text. It involves extracting subjective information from the text and classifying it as positive, negative, or neutral.

Early sentiment analysis techniques mostly relied on lexicons, which are predefined lists of words annotated with sentiment scores. These lexicons cataloged words and phrases along with their polarities, often by crowdsourcing human annotators. One such well-known lexicon is the AFINN lexicon, which assigns polarity scores ranging from -5 to +5 to words based on their sentiment.

By summing up the sentiment scores of individual words in a piece of text, these techniques could estimate the overall sentiment conveyed.

However, relying solely on lexicons had several limitations. Their effectiveness greatly depends on the context in which words are being used and their inherent ambiguity. Polysemy, where a word can possess multiple meanings, was one such challenge to tackle. For example, the word "cool" could denote a positive sentiment when used to describe something impressive, but it could also convey a negative sentiment when used sarcastically.

To address these challenges, other methods were developed, including the use of machine learning models. Supervised learning algorithms, such as Support Vector Machines (SVM), Decision Trees, and Naive Bayes classifiers, enabled automatic sentiment analysis by learning from labeled datasets. These models extracted features from the text, such as word frequencies or syntactic patterns, and utilized them to classify the sentiment.

Additionally, researchers explored the incorporation of linguistic knowledge into sentiment analysis. Techniques like part-of-speech tagging and syntactic parsing helped in capturing the dependency relationships between words in a sentence, providing a more nuanced understanding of sentiments expressed. Additionally, sentiment lexicons were expanded to include phrases, idiomatic expressions, and even emojis that convey emotions.

While these traditional approaches showed promise in gauging emotional undercurrents, they faced limitations in handling complex linguistic constructions, sarcasm, irony, and detecting subtle context-dependent emotions. As a result, researchers turned their attention towards more advanced techniques, such as deep learning, which have been shown to outperform these traditional approaches in various NLP tasks.

As the field of NLP continues to evolve, traditional approaches act as stepping stones, paving the way for more sophisticated methods that harness the power of machine learning and neural networks. The quest to accurately determine emotional undercurrents within texts remains an ongoing journey, as researchers explore new data sources, develop innovative algorithms, and deepen their understanding of human emotions and linguistic nuances.

8.2 Deep Learning Insights: Mining Emotion in Text

Understanding and interpreting human emotions from text has always been a fascinating challenge for researchers and practitioners in the field of Natural Language Processing. As language plays a significant role in reflecting our emotions, being able to mine emotions from text holds immense potential in various domains, from sentiment analysis in social media to mental health monitoring and customer feedback analysis. In recent years, deep learning techniques have emerged as powerful tools for unlocking a deeper understanding of emotions encoded within textual data.

Emotion mining, also known as sentiment analysis or affective computing, primarily aims to identify and categorize the emotions conveyed by individuals through their written words. Traditional approaches to sentiment analysis often relied on handcrafted features, such as keyword extraction or bag-of-words representations, combined with rule-based classifiers. While these techniques might yield moderate results on standard datasets, they often fall short when dealing with the complexity and nuances of human emotions.

Deep learning methods, on the other hand, have revolutionized the field of natural language processing by automatically learning meaningful representations from raw text data. These neural network-based models excel at capturing intricate patterns and relationships between words, which are crucial for accurate emotion mining. By creating deep neural architectures capable of modeling more abstract concepts and contextual dependencies, researchers have been able to tackle the challenges of extracting emotions from text with greater precision and robustness.

One of the core ingredients in deep learning models for emotion mining is the use of word embeddings. Word embeddings are dense vector representations that capture semantic and syntactic similarities between words. These embeddings allow neural networks to understand the contextual information encoded in sentences or documents, enabling them to differentiate between subtle variations of sentiment and emotion.

Deep learning insights into emotion mining involve various architectures, including recurrent neural networks (RNNs), convolutional neural networks (CNNs), and more recent models like transformers. RNNs, specifically long short-term memory (LSTM) networks, have demonstrated great success in capturing sequential dependencies in text, making them well-suited for sentiment analysis tasks. CNNs, on the other hand, excel at learning local patterns and extracting feature maps, making them popular for emotion mining in texts. Transformers, represented by models like BERT, have introduced attention mechanisms that enable the encoding of important information from both preceding and succeeding contexts, resulting in impressive state-of-the-art performance on a wide range of NLP tasks.

As the field advances, researchers are now leveraging multimodal approaches that combine textual information with additional modalities such as images and audio. By incorporating non-verbal cues present in multimodal data, deep learning models can capture emotions with greater accuracy and expressiveness. This intersection of deep learning with multimodal emotion mining holds great potential for applications in areas like virtual assistants, healthcare, and market research.

In conclusion, deep learning insights have revolutionized the field of emotion mining in text by allowing models to learn nuanced contextual representations and capture complex emotional signals. From utilizing word embeddings to incorporating multimodal data, researchers continue to push the boundaries of emotion mining using various deep learning architectures. As the field progresses, new approaches and techniques will emerge, enabling us to gain a deeper understanding of human emotions encoded within text data and opening doors to exciting applications in numerous domains.

8.3 Aspect-Based Analysis: Deconstructing Sentiment Complexity

In the world of Natural Language Processing (NLP), the ability to analyze and understand sentiment expressed in text is a crucial task. Traditionally, sentiment analysis has focused on determining whether a given text expresses positive, negative, or neutral sentiment overall. However, in real-world applications, sentiment can be much more nuanced and multi-faceted. Aspect-Based Analysis (ABA) is emerging as a powerful technique to unravel the complexities of sentiment by deconstructing it into various aspects or subtopics.

8.3 Aspect-Based Analysis: Deconstructing Sentiment Complexity

1. Understanding Aspects

Aspect-Based Analysis revolves around the concept of aspects. Aspects refer to specific areas, features, or attributes of an entity or subject being analyzed. In sentiment analysis, aspects can be thought of as the building blocks that help increase the granularity and specificity of sentiment expression. For example, when analyzing restaurant reviews, aspects could include the food quality, service, ambience, or prices.

2. Importance of Aspect-Based Analysis

ABA is essential because it enables a more detailed understanding of sentiment. By breaking down a text into aspects, analysts gain insights into what aspects of a subject and which sentiments are associated with them. This information is valuable for businesses, researchers, or any analysis focused on improving specific elements or understanding customer experiences in greater detail.

3. The Challenges of Aspect Extraction

One of the main challenges in Aspect-Based Analysis lies in accurately identifying aspects within a given text. Unlike overall sentiment analysis, where the polarity is studied at a document or sentence level, aspect extraction demands a deeper understanding of the subject and the ability to identify relevant aspects accurately.

Implementation aspect extraction techniques can vary significantly, from rule-based approaches that rely on predefined linguistic patterns to more advanced methods involving machine learning and deep learning techniques. Researchers are continuously exploring new techniques and improving existing ones to tackle the challenge of aspect extraction effectively.

4. Aspect-Based Sentiment Analysis

Once aspects are identified, aspect-based sentiment analysis focuses on understanding the sentiment expressed towards each aspect. Entailed within this phase, sentiment polarity is attributed to individual aspects, revealing more nuanced and detailed sentiment information than traditional sentiment analysis.

One common approach to aspect-based sentiment analysis involves utilizing sentiment lexicons or sentiment dictionaries, which contain precomputed sentiment scores or polarities for words corresponding to different emotions. These resources allow analysts to assign sentiment polarities to aspects based on the semantic orientation of associated words. Machine learning techniques, such as supervised or unsupervised approaches, are also employed in aspect-based sentiment analysis to make sentiment predictions based on training data.

5. Challenges in Aspect-Based Sentiment Analysis

Aspect-Based Sentiment Analysis is not without its challenges. It involves addressing issues like aspect ambiguity, contextual sentiment variation, and the lack of annotated data. Identifying dominant aspects, resolving aspect conflicts, and adequately capturing aspect-specific sentiment nuances further add to the complexity of this analysis.

Researchers continue to explore innovative techniques to overcome these challenges, including incorporating contextual information, contextual word embeddings, or leveraging other external resources such as knowledge graphs or ontologies to enhance the accuracy of aspect-based sentiment analysis.

Conclusion

Entailed within this section of the book, we have explored aspect-based analysis as a technique for deconstructing sentiment complexity in Natural Language Processing. By understanding aspects and their relevance to sentiment analysis, we can gain insights into more specific aspects of a subject and their associated sentiments. We have also acknowledged the challenges involved in aspect extraction and aspect-based sentiment analysis and highlighted ongoing research efforts to address these challenges effectively. Aspect-Based Analysis paves the way for a deeper understanding and a more nuanced interpretation of sentiments expressed in text, benefiting various applications, businesses, and researchers.

8.4 Ethical Considerations: Navigating the Sentimental Landscape

As Natural Language Processing (NLP) continues to advance and impact various aspects of our society, it becomes crucial to explore the ethical considerations associated with this technology. Navigating the sentimental landscape of NLP involves understanding and addressing the ethical challenges that arise in the field.

One of the primary ethical concerns in NLP is bias, whether in the data used for training models, the algorithms themselves, or the output generated. NLP systems inherit biases present in the data they are trained on, which can perpetuate societal biases and discrimination. For example, if a sentiment analysis model is trained on a predominantly biased dataset, it may disproportionately classify certain groups or individuals negatively or unfairly. To alleviate this issue, researchers and practitioners are increasingly focusing on bias mitigation techniques to make NLP algorithms more fair and unbiased. This includes upstream work like carefully curating training datasets to be representative and reducing bias, as well as developing fairness metrics and strategies for debiasing models. Understanding and quantifying bias in NLP systems is pivotal in striving for fairness and equality.

Another pressing ethical consideration lies in the privacy and security aspects of NLP. Language processing often involves analyzing textual data, which might include personal and sensitive information. There is a risk of unintended exposure and potential misuse of this data that can lead to serious consequences, such as identity theft or violation of privacy laws. Researchers and practitioners must incorporate measures for data anonymization, encryption, and secure storage to ensure the protection of individuals' private information.

Moreover, the democratization and widespread adoption of NLP tools also raise concerns about the potential for misuse or malicious intent. For instance, sentiment analysis, if used unethically, could be employed to manipulate public opinion or engage in online harassment campaigns. Therefore, regulatory frameworks and ethical guidelines should be established to prevent the misuse of NLP technology and safeguard against its harmful effects.

On the flip side, it is essential to consider the impact of NLP on cultural and linguistic diversity. Natural language is not universal, varying across communities, dialects, and languages. When developing NLP systems, it is crucial to include a broad range of cultural perspectives and linguistic diversity, avoiding the undue dominance of any specific language or culture. Failure to do so may result in marginalization or exclusion of certain groups, reinforcing power imbalances and perpetuating inequalities.

Proactive engagement with stakeholders, including users, activists, academics, and industry experts, is vital in shaping the ethical landscape of NLP. Open dialogues and collaborations can help identify and address socio-ethical concerns, mitigate biases in datasets, and establish guidelines for the use of NLP in sensitive applications. Rich interdisciplinary collaboration between computer scientists, ethicists, sociologists, linguists, and policy experts is necessary to build a comprehensive ethical framework for NLP that considers the interests and welfare of all stakeholders involved.

In conclusion, venturing into the sentimental landscape of NLP requires navigating a multitude of ethical considerations. Addressing bias, ensuring privacy and security, preventing malicious use, promoting cultural diversity, and fostering stakeholder engagement are crucial steps in shaping an ethical and responsible future for NLP. As this technology continues to evolve, it is in the best interest of the community to prioritize ethical considerations, balancing advancements with considerations of societal well-being.

Chapter 9: Bridging Language Divides

9.1 Rule-based Translation: The Bridge of Linguistic Convergence

Language has always been a powerful form of communication, serving as a bridge of understanding between people from different cultures and backgrounds. As the world becomes more interconnected and globalized, the need for effective translation and Natural Language Processing (NLP) has grown exponentially. Engulfed by this chapter, we will explore one of the fundamental concepts of NLP: rule-based translation.

Rule-based translation involves the use of predefined linguistic rules to convert text from one language into another. These rules are created by linguists and language experts who have deep knowledge of both the source and target languages. It is through the meticulous analysis of grammatical structures, syntax, and vocabulary that these rules are developed.

The underlying principle behind rule-based translation is the belief that languages share a common structure, or what we call linguistic convergence. This means that languages, despite their differences, can be systematically mapped onto one another with the help of linguistic rules. These rules are designed to capture the unique characteristics of each language, enabling accurate and meaningful translations to take place.

To begin with, rule-based translation requires an extensive linguistic analysis of both the source and target languages. This analysis helps identify patterns and regularities, which are then encoded into a set of rules. These rules outline how various linguistic elements, such as nouns, verbs, adjectives, and grammatical constructions, can be translated and integrated into the target language.

In rule-based translation systems, the rules dictate not only the mapping of words from one language to another but also the transformation of sentence structures to maintain semantic coherence. For example, in English-to-French translation, the rule might specify that the subject should precede the verb in the translated sentence, in contrast to the English sentence structure where the subject typically follows the verb.

Creating such rules involves both the identification of linguistic equivalences and the recognition of linguistic variations. This requires a deep understanding of both the source and target languages, including their grammatical rules, idiomatic expressions, and cultural nuances. The aim is to create rules that accurately capture the meaning and nuances of the original text and convey them faithfully in the translated version.

Rule-based translation systems, though highly accurate when applied to well-defined languages and domains, do have limitations. Firstly, since the rules are manually crafted, the process can be time-consuming and labor-intensive. Secondly, rule-based systems struggle to handle languages with significant structural differences or complex idiomatic expressions that do not have direct equivalents in the target language.

However, advancements in NLP research have attempted to address these challenges. Machine learning algorithms and statistical models have been incorporated to enhance rule-based translation systems. By analyzing vast amounts of bilingual data and identifying patterns within them automatically, these models help improve the accuracy and robustness of translations.

In conclusion, rule-based translation stands as a crucial pillar of NLP for beginners. It provides a principled framework for resolving the intricacies of languages and bridging the linguistic gap between cultures. While rule-based translation systems have their limitations, they lay the foundation for further research and development in the field. As the world continues to shrink and communication becomes more diverse, the quest for more effective and accurate machine translation systems continues to evolve.

9.2 Statistical Translation: The Symphony of Multilingualism

As explorers of language, we find ourselves marveling at the sheer beauty and complexity of multilingualism. Humans have been communicating across different languages for centuries, creating a rich tapestry of diverse cultures and knowledge. While this linguistic diversity fosters intellectual growth and cultural exchanges, it also poses significant challenges when trying to bridge the gap between different languages.

In recent years, Natural Language Processing (NLP) has emerged as a field of study dedicated to understanding and generating human language using computational techniques. One fundamental problem that NLP tackles is statistical translation, a method that aims to enable communication between languages through machine learning algorithms.

Statistical translation goes beyond mere word-to-word substitution; it seeks to comprehend the underlying meaning, nuances, and cultural connotations of a given sentence in one language and convey it accurately in another. Just like a symphony requires the harmonious integration of various musical instruments to create a melody, statistical translation employs a complex blend of statistical models and linguistic analysis techniques to create a beautiful symphony of words across different languages.

At the heart of statistical translation lies the concept of alignment, where associations are established between words or phrases in different languages. These associations become building blocks to construct translation models capable of generating fluent phrases in the target language. Achieving an accurate alignment is akin to tuning the instruments of our symphony—each word, phrase, and sentence buildup complements the others, resulting in a seamless translation.

Understanding this symphony from an NLP perspective involves breaking down the language process into smaller statistical building blocks. One key technique employed is the use of parallel data, large bilingual corpora that act as a bridge between different languages. These corpora are meticulously annotated with word alignments or phrase correspondences, assisting in creating the necessary statistical models for translation. This allows for the automatic identification of linguistic patterns, helping machines comprehend and recreate the intricate dance of multilingualism.

Another crucial aspect is the application of statistical machine learning algorithms, shaped by Nobel laureate Claude Shannon's theory of information. These algorithms learn from the parallel data, enabling them to make intelligent decisions about translating new unseen sentences. Through the magic of probabilistic models, our machines identify patterns and uncover statistical regularities inherent within the source and target languages, allowing them to approximate the true meaning of human expression.

However, statistical translation is not without pitfalls. The symphony of multilingualism is shaped by dynamic forces, cultural specificities, and even dialectical variations that make each language distinct. Ambiguities concealed within sentences and subtle cultural references are like moments of disharmony that interrupt our symphony. To overcome these hurdles, researchers continuously strive to refine statistical models and explore newer techniques like syntactic and semantic representations of language. These advancements aim to enhance the accuracy and fluidity of translation, bringing us closer to the dream of seamless multilingual communication.

The pursuit of statistical translation represents an exquisite endeavor, blending the art of language with the power of computational algorithms. As beginners venturing into the fascinating world of NLP, we embark on a journey to reveal the true nature of language, understanding its nuances, and unlocking the hidden gems of multilingualism. With time, perseverance, and continuous improvement, we strive to create symphonies that traverse the boundaries of languages, uniting people in the harmonious exchange of ideas and culture.

9.3 Neural Translation: Redefining Cross-Cultural Communication

As society becomes increasingly globalized, there is a growing need for efficient and accurate cross-cultural communication. Humans have long relied on translation services to bridge linguistic barriers, but these services are often time-consuming and prone to error. However, thanks to advancements in technology, particularly in the field of Natural Language Processing (NLP), researchers are now redefining the way we approach translation.

In the vast field of NLP, one area that has garnered significant attention is neural translation. Neural translation, also known as machine translation, is a branch of NLP that focuses on developing algorithms capable of automatically translating text from one language to another. Unlike traditional rule-based translation systems that required explicit instructions and large amounts of linguistic information, neural translation takes a more data-driven approach, relying on large-scale training datasets and advanced machine learning techniques.

At the heart of neural translation lies the neural network, a computational model that seeks to simulate the behavior of the human brain. These networks are designed to learn patterns and relationships in various data inputs, enabling them to generate accurate translations. One of the key advantages of this approach is its ability to capture the nuances of language and better understand context, resulting in more natural and human-like translations.

To train a neural translation system, one must compile a vast amount of bilingual data. This data consists of pairs of sentences in multiple languages, with each pair representing a translation. These datasets can be obtained from various sources, such as publicly available parallel corpora or language-specific databases. However, the quality and size of the dataset play a crucial role in the performance of the neural translation system.

Once the dataset is compiled, the neural network is trained using state-of-the-art techniques such as recurrent neural networks (RNNs) or transformer models. These models analyze the input text, encoding the information into a numerical representation known as embeddings. These embeddings are then fed into a decoding layer, which generates the output translation. The neural network iteratively adjusts its parameters during the training process, minimizing the errors between the generated translations and the ground truth translations in the dataset.

While neural translation has shown tremendous progress in recent years, it is not without its challenges. One major issue is the scarcity of high-quality bilingual training data for certain language pairs or low-resource languages. This lack of data hampers the performance of the translation system and leads to subpar translations. Additionally, there are difficulties in translating idiomatic expressions, colloquialisms, and cultural references that may not have direct translations in another language.

To overcome these challenges, researchers are constantly exploring innovative techniques. This includes the use of transfer learning, where a neural translation model trained on large-scale, high-resource languages is fine-tuned for low-resource languages. Another approach involves incorporating contextual information and cultural knowledge into the neural network, enabling it to make more informed translation decisions.

In conclusion, neural translation has revolutionized the field of cross-cultural communication. Through the utilization of advanced machine learning techniques and vast datasets, researchers have made significant strides in creating more accurate and natural translations. As technology continues to advance, and the field of NLP continues to evolve, we can anticipate even further improvements in neural translation, redefining the way we communicate globally.

9.4 Quality Assessment: Ensuring Linguistic Fidelity

As we journey into the world of Natural Language Processing (NLP), it is crucial to understand the importance of maintaining linguistic fidelity within our models and systems. Ensuring that our NLP solutions accurately represent the intricacies of human language is essential for achieving meaningful and valuable results. Engulfed by this section, we will delve into the concept of quality assessment in NLP and explore various approaches to guarantee linguistic fidelity.

Linguistic fidelity refers to the degree to which an NLP model or system captures the nuances, grammar, vocabulary, and contextual meaning inherent in human language. It encompasses the accurate interpretation of natural language utterances, maintaining syntactic and semantic structure, and preserving the original intent and coherence of the text. As the demand for NLP solutions grows, so does the need to develop reliable methods to assess and measure the linguistic fidelity of these systems.

Quality assessment represents a pivotal step in the NLP pipeline. Before deploying an NLP system or model, it is crucial to thoroughly evaluate its performance and ensure linguistic fidelity. Engulfed by this process, various techniques can be employed to simulate real-world scenarios and scrutinize the outputs generated by the NLP system.

One prevalent approach to quality assessment is the use of human annotators. Through carefully designed annotation tasks and guidelines, human evaluators thoroughly examine the system's performance by assessing its responses for accuracy, fluency, and overall linguistic coherence. These evaluations enable the identification of any discrepancies or inadequacies in the system's responses, allowing for necessary adjustments to maintain linguistic fidelity.

Additionally, automated evaluation metrics can provide valuable insights into the linguistic quality of an NLP system. These metrics gauge the effectiveness of the system by comparing its output against a reference or gold-standard corpus. Common metrics include BLEU (Bilingual Evaluation Understudy) and ROUGE (Recall-Oriented Understudy for Gisting Evaluation), which measure the n-gram overlap between generated text and human references. While these metrics offer quantitative measures of performance, they often fail to capture the intricacies of language and may not address linguistic fidelity comprehensively.

Another critical component of quality assessment revolves around adversarial testing. Adversarial testing involves subjecting the NLP system to challenging scenarios that mimic real-world usage. This technique aims to uncover potential weaknesses, biases, limitations, or unintended behaviors of the NLP system. By simulating a variety of linguistic variations, figurative language, ambiguous expressions, or rare use cases, researchers can identify areas where the system lacks linguistic fidelity and work toward enhancements.

Ethical considerations are also paramount when assessing the quality and linguistic fidelity of NLP solutions. Evaluators should be aware of potential biases in training data, inappropriate responses, offensive language, or content that may be distressing for users. It is crucial to integrate mechanisms that ensure fairness, inclusivity, and respect for diverse cultures and perspectives in NLP systems.

Furthermore, ongoing evaluation and continuous improvement are key for sustaining linguistic fidelity. As language evolves and new challenges arise, NLP systems should be regularly assessed and adapted to maintain their performance and linguistic accuracy. Establishing a feedback loop that includes user feedback, error analysis, and fine-tuning of the underlying models is essential for quality assessment and addressing any linguistic fidelity issues.

In conclusion, ensuring linguistic fidelity is crucial in Natural Language Processing. Quality assessment plays a fundamental role in evaluating and perfecting NLP systems to accurately capture the complexity and authenticity of human language. By leveraging human evaluations, automated metrics, adversarial testing, and ethical considerations, researchers and developers can enhance the linguistic fidelity of NLP solutions, ultimately advancing the field and creating meaningful interactions between humans and machines.

Chapter 10: Textual Artistry: Generating Narratives

10.1 Rule-based Generation: Weaving Stories with Logic

As humans, storytelling is an inherent part of our nature. We have been passing down stories from generation to generation, transporting ourselves into unique worlds created by the imagination of those who came before us. But what if we could teach machines to create such stories, tales that captivate and immerse the reader in a universe of their making?

Natural Language Processing (NLP) is the branch of artificial intelligence concerned with the interaction between computers and human language. It encompasses a multitude of techniques and algorithms designed to enable computers to understand, interpret, and generate human language. Rule-based generation is one such technique within the realm of NLP that attempts to simulate the art of storytelling.

Rule-based generation leverages logical rules to construct coherent and engaging narratives. These rules allow the machine to piece together various elements, such as characters, settings, and events, to create a cohesive story structure. Just as an author would carefully craft a narrative using a set of predefined rules, the machine formulates its stories based on a pre-existing framework.

To achieve rule-based generation, one must establish a set of rules that dictate the relationships between different narrative components. For example, a rule could state that "if the protagonist is in a dangerous situation, then the antagonist will emerge." By implementing logical conditions like these, the machine can meticulously construct a storyline that aligns with the desired plot progression.

The success of rule-based generation lies in the implementation of these rules and the execution of logical structures. This process requires a deep understanding of human storytelling conventions, narrative arcs, and character development. It also entails meticulous analysis of existing works of literature to distill the underlying patterns and frameworks that shape compelling stories. Novice researchers venturing into the field of NLP and rule-based generation can begin by exploring literature, both classic and contemporary. Studying renowned authors and analyzing their narrative techniques will help familiarize beginners with the prevalent story structures and their underlying logic. This exposure also aids in identifying patterns and recurring motifs, which are essential in developing effective rules for story generation.

Simultaneously, immersion in the world of linguistics and computational linguistics plays a crucial role in grasping the fundamentals of NLP. Understanding the intricacies of grammar, syntax, and semantics equips researchers with the tools needed to design rules that generate grammatically correct and syntactically coherent narratives.

While rule-based generation offers a structured approach to story creation, it is worth noting that the success of such systems heavily relies on the richness and diversity of the established rules. Researchers must continuously refine and expand their rule sets to encompass a broader range of storytelling possibilities. Additionally, incorporating machine learning techniques into rule-based systems can enhance the adaptability and sophistication of the generated narratives.

Embarking upon the journey of learning and researching rule-based generation for NLP requires equal parts creativity, logical thinking, and a deep appreciation for storytelling. As beginners delve into this realm, they will discover the interconnectedness of the human mind, language, and the art of constructing captivating narratives. Through their studies, they will learn the alchemy of weaving stories with logic, bridging the gap between human imagination and the logic-driven world of machines.

10.2 Template-driven Narratives: The Palette of Templates

Templates are the backbone of modern natural language processing (NLP) systems for generating coherent and natural-sounding narratives. A template can be thought of as a fill-in-the-blank sentence structure that provides a framework for generating text. The use of templates in NLP allows for the creation of narratives that are contextual, engaging, and responsive to user input.

In template-driven narratives, the focus lies on the ability to generate text that fits within predefined patterns. These patterns encompass a wide range of possibilities, from simple sentence structures to complex story plots. The palette of templates available to NLP systems forms a starting point for constructing narratives, providing a framework that guides the generation process.

The flexibility of template-driven narratives makes them suitable for a diverse range of applications. They can be utilized in chatbots, virtual assistants, customer service systems, and even in video game dialogue. The key advantage of using templates is that they can be easily modified and expanded upon, enabling developers to create rich and dynamic narratives without starting from scratch.

To harness the power of template-driven narratives, researchers often resort to statistical and machine learning techniques. These methodologies involve training models on large amounts of textual data to learn patterns and create reliable generators. Statistical models such as n-gram language models or neural network-based approaches are commonly employed within NLP systems to ensure the generation of coherent and contextually appropriate text.

The process of constructing templates involves careful consideration of linguistic factors like syntax, semantics, and discourse structure. For example, a template used for dialogue between two characters should accurately reflect the patterns and manners of human conversation. Similarly, a template designed for generating informative paragraphs should demonstrate a strong grasp of topic transitions and coherence.

Given the multitude of possibilities, building a comprehensive palette of templates requires extensive research and analysis. Researchers embark on extensive dataset exploration and linguistic analysis to identify prevalent patterns and structures within the genre or domain they are working on. By closely studying existing narratives and examining linguistic phenomena, they endeavor to uncover the inherent principles that govern storytelling and refine the templates accordingly.

Once the templates have been crafted and refined, NLP systems employ various algorithms to select and populate slots within the templates. These slots act as placeholders for dynamic and context-specific information, allowing the generated narratives to adapt and respond to user prompts or changing circumstances.

From a broader perspective, template-driven narratives highlight the interplay between creativity and structure in language production. While templates provide a scaffolding for generating text, they also open up possibilities for creative expression within predetermined boundaries. Balancing the need for coherent narrative flow with the desire for diversity and richness of content is a delicate task that researchers in the field of NLP continually strive to improve upon.

In conclusion, templates serve as building blocks for constructing natural-sounding and contextually intelligent narratives in NLP systems. Ranging from simple sentence structures to complex story plots, templates offer a versatile toolkit for generating coherent text. By combining statistical and machine learning techniques with linguistic analysis, researchers can create robust NLP models capable of generating narrative texts that are responsive, engaging, and aligned with the objectives of the application. The utilization of templates and the construction of a diverse palette present exciting avenues for exploration and improvement in the field of NLP.

10.3 Recurrent Neural Networks: The Poets of the Digital Age

With advancements in Natural Language Processing, also known as NLP, researchers are constantly exploring new techniques to understand and generate human language with machines. One such technique that has gained significant attention in recent years is the use of Recurrent Neural Networks (RNNs).

RNNs are unique neural networks that are well-suited for processing sequential data, such as language. Unlike traditional feedforward neural networks, which only operate on fixed-length inputs, RNNs maintain an internal state that enables them to process variable-length sequences. This makes them intriguing models for tasks like language modeling, machine translation, sentiment analysis, and even poetry generation.

If we consider language as a structured series of words, phrases, and sentences, an RNN can be envisioned as an unfolding chain where each link in the chain denotes the occurrence of a word or phrase. This unfolding chain signifies the recurrent nature of the network, meaning that it can capture not only the current input but also consider the context from previous inputs. This attribute makes RNNs especially effective for tasks that require understanding dependencies and temporal dynamics in data.

When it comes to language generation, RNNs have proven to be the poets of the digital age. By leveraging their ability to model sequences, RNNs can be trained on vast amounts of text data to learn patterns, structures, and semantic relationships within sentences and paragraphs. Once trained, RNNs can generate text that mimics the styles and characteristics exhibited by the training data, even spilling into the realm of creating poems.

Researchers have developed various flavors of RNNs, each with its own unique properties and architectures. For instance, the most basic type of RNN is called a vanilla RNN, which suffers from the notorious "vanishing gradient" problem during training. To overcome this limitation, different variants such as Long Short-Term Memory (LSTM) and Gated Recurrent Unit (GRU) have been devised, which alleviate the vanishing gradient problem and enable training of deeper RNN models.

Furthermore, researchers have gone beyond traditional RNNs and introduced innovative architectures, like Attention-based RNNs, which focus specifically on attending to specific parts of the input sequence while generating outputs. Attention mechanisms have enhanced the capability of RNN models, allowing them to capture more context and generate more coherent and contextually appropriate text.

However, it is important to note that despite their exceptional performance, RNNs are not without their challenges. One common challenge arises from the trade-off between modeling long-term dependencies and maintaining computational efficiency. Training RNNs, particularly on large datasets, can require significant computational resources and time due to their sequential nature.

Another challenge stems from the quality and diversity of training data. RNNs heavily rely on the input data they are trained on, meaning that if the training data is biased or limited, the generated texts may also exhibit biases or lack diversity. Researchers are continuously working to overcome these challenges, developing methods to improve the robustness, creative potential, and ethical aspects of RNN-based language generation models.

In conclusion, Recurrent Neural Networks have revolutionized Natural Language Processing and opened up exciting possibilities for language understanding and generation. By leveraging their unique ability to capture sequential dependencies, RNNs have become proficient in mimicking the prowess of human poets, presenting a fascinating direction in the evolution of computational creativity. As researchers delve deeper into these models, it is expected that they will continue to refine and enhance RNNs, pushing the boundaries of what can be achieved in the realm of language-based artificial intelligence.

10.4 Transformer-based Generation: Crafting Textual Epics

The Transformers model is a breakthrough in NLP, especially in tasks such as machine translation, text summarization, and question-answering. Among this chapter, however, we specifically explore its application in text generation. More precisely, we are interested in crafting textual epics – compelling narratives that captivate and enchant readers.

To comprehend the essence of crafting textual epics, we must first understand the core principles of the Transformers model. The Transformers architecture revolutionized the field of NLP by introducing the concept of self-attention mechanisms. Unlike earlier models that relied on recurrent or convolutional neural networks, Transformers rely solely on attention mechanisms to capture dependencies between words in a sequence. This allows them to have a broad contextual understanding of the text, resulting in superior performance in various NLP tasks.

For the purposes of generating textual epics, we employ specific variations of the baseline Transformers model. One commonly used method is the conditional or autoregressive generation, in which the model predicts the next word based on the context of the previous words. This process is repeated iteratively to craft long and captivating narratives. Another intriguing approach is non-autoregressive generation, in which we aim to generate the full text at once. While this poses several challenges, such as maintaining coherence, it has shown promise in certain settings.

To apply the Transformers model to generate textual epics, we require a substantial corpus of training data. Here, large-scale text datasets become invaluable, providing a diverse range of writing styles, topics, and perspectives. These datasets enable the model to learn the intricacies of language and create truly unique storylines.

As with any text generation task, evaluation becomes essential to judge the success of our AI-generated epics. Metrics such as perplexity and diversity provide quantitative measures of the generated text's quality. Moreover, human evaluations play a crucial role in assessing the subjective aspects of storytelling. By collecting feedback from readers, we gain insight into various aspects like coherence, engagement, and overall satisfaction.

Beyond the technicalities, the true essence of crafting textual epics lies in the creativity and artistry involved. Just like human authors, AI models can learn to evoke emotions, build complex characters, and weave intricate plotlines. From fantasy realms filled with magic and enchantment to dystopian futures teeming with technological marvels, the possibilities are limitless. By fostering creativity and narrative craftsmanship within the field of NLP, we unlock new dimensions for AI-generated storytelling.

In conclusion, the 10.4 Transformer-based Generation: Crafting Textual Epics chapter ushers beginners into the world of generating captivating textual narratives using transformer-based models. With the advent of Transformers and its attention mechanisms, AI models can create long and immersive textual epics, showcasing the tremendous potential of NLP. As we continue to explore text generation and push its boundaries, the power of storytelling through AI takes center stage, demonstrating the incredible capabilities of natural language processing.

Chapter 11: Navigating the Information Seas

11.1 The Information Odyssey: Charting Knowledge Realms

In the ever-expanding realm of Artificial Intelligence (AI), Natural Language Processing (NLP) stands out as a fascinating field that continues to garner immense interest and research. With its potential to bridge the gap between humans and machines by enabling computers to comprehend and communicate human language, NLP has opened up new avenues for countless applications such as chatbots, virtual assistants, sentiment analysis, machine translation, and much more.

As a beginner embarking on a journey to understand and delve into the foundations of NLP, it becomes crucial to embrace the art of researching this extensive domain. Delving into the world of NLP research is akin to embarking on an information odyssey. Each path one takes from language understanding to text generation, from sentiment analysis to named entity recognition, unfolds a plethora of resources and techniques waiting to be explored and assimilated.

To navigate this miraculous realm successfully, one must develop a keen pursuant of knowledge acquisition through rigorous research practices. The process of researching NLP necessitates an inquisitive mindset willing to explore the wisdom imparted by academic papers, scholarly articles, research journals, conference proceedings, and the achievements of both renowned and aspiring individuals in the field.

In essence, the journey to becoming proficient in NLP involves mastering the art of information gathering, analysis, and synthesis. Firstly, one must acquaint oneself with the key terminology associated with NLP, ensuring that foundational concepts such as tokenization, part-of-speech tagging, syntactic parsing, and semantic understanding are comprehended with meticulous detail.

Once a solid foundation is established, the aspiring NLP researcher must then venture into the vast array of research papers and books available. These sources function as signposts on the information odyssey path, guiding one towards essential frameworks and methodologies proven effective in solving intricate language-related problems. Diligently studying these texts, drawing connections between related research breakthroughs, and critically analyzing existing approaches will solidify one's understanding of the subject matter.

In addition to traditional academic resources, exploring the vast online NLP community brings immense value to an eager researcher. Online forums, discussion boards, and dedicated websites provide a platform for knowledge-sharing, problem-solving, and fostering collaborations. Engaging in discussions, seeking guidance, and sharing insights will further accelerate the learning process while providing an opportunity to build a supportive network of fellow enthusiasts and researchers.

Moreover, as the field of NLP progresses at a relentless pace, it is quintessential to stay up-to-date with the latest advancements. Following academic conferences, such as the Association for Computational Linguistics (ACL), the Conference on Empirical Methods in Natural Language Processing (EMNLP), and the North American Chapter of the Association for Computational Linguistics (NAACL), allows researchers to tap into the collective accomplishments of the global NLP community.

While these conferences provide a snapshot of the state of the field, it is essential to embrace continuous learning through online courses, tutorials, and workshops. Platforms such as Coursera, edX, and YouTube offer abundant resources that cover a wide range of NLP topics, accommodating various skill levels. Completing these courses helps to gain practical knowledge and hands-on experience, enabling researchers to apply theories to real-world problems.

To flourish in the NLP domain, it is crucial to cultivate originality and innovation. Thinking outside the box and questioning established paradigms fuel the development of groundbreaking approaches and algorithms. By daring to challenge existing techniques or proposing novel methodologies, one can not only contribute to the collective intelligence of the NLP discipline but also take personal growth and knowledge acquisition to new heights.

Indeed, stepping into the realm of NLP research is akin to embarking on a wondrous information odyssey. By honing the art of research, diligently exploring academic papers and conferences, actively participating in online communities, staying abreast of cutting-edge advancements, and nurturing a mindset of innovation, one can embark on an exhilarating journey that will unlock extraordinary possibilities in the world of NLP. May this expedition serve as a gateway to unlocking the hidden potential of human-computer interaction, propelling the boundaries of AI ever further.

11.2 Inverted Indexing: Unveiling Textual Treasure Troves

Imagine a vast library, filled with countless books, each containing a wealth of information. At first glance, it may be overwhelming, as finding a specific piece of knowledge within this immense sea of books seems like an arduous task. However, fear not! Inverted indexing equips us with a potent tool that brings order to this great chaos.

The concept of inverted indexing begins with recognizing that an index can simplify our search for specific terms or entities in a document collection. Traditionally, the index allows us to find documents that contain certain words. However, the inverted index takes this concept further by mapping each word to a list of documents that contain it.

To understand this process better, let's grasp the essence of inverted indexing through a practical example. Suppose we have a library with five books: A, B, C, D, and E. The words and sentences played by these books form our textual treasure troves. When we create an inverted index for this mini-library, its structure may resemble something like this:

Word | Documents

|-

NLP | A, B, E

indexing | A, B, D

treasure | A, C, D

troves | C, E

In our little library, the term "NLP" appears in books A, B, and E. The term "indexing" can be found in books A, B, and D. Similarly, "treasure" lurks within books A, C, and D, while "troves" can be spotted in books C and E.

By building an inverted index, we go beyond simply knowing whether a document contains a specific word. We gain a highly organized structure that allows us to locate both the documents containing a term and the terms that exist within specific documents. This grants us the power to unveil connections, patterns, and insights that were previously hidden amidst the textual sea.

Now let's consider how we can implement this concept efficiently. Suppose we have a large collection of documents, and our goal is to create an inverted index for them. The process can be broken down into three key steps:

1. Tokenization: We first break down each document into individual words (tokens). This helps us create a list of unique terms present in the collection.

2. Document Indexing: Now, for each unique term, we create a list of documents that contain it. This involves traversing through the documents and identifying the presence of each term.

3. Search and Retrieval: Once the inverted index is created, we can swiftly search for terms or entities and retrieve the related documents or sections containing those terms.

Inverted indexing, with its ability to unmask hidden knowledge, expands the boundaries of traditional search techniques. It allows us to explore textual data from a whole new perspective, accelerating our journey toward unraveling information and drawing meaningful insights.

Now armed with this newfound knowledge, we stand ready to further explore and experiment with inverted indexing, forging ahead confidently in our quest to conquer the complex and fascinating realm of Natural Language Processing.

11.3 Retrieval Models: Finding Needles in the Digital Haystack

The world we live in today is inundated with an enormous amount of digital information. From books and articles to social media posts and emails, the proliferation of data on the internet is staggering. As a result, finding relevant information amidst this vast sea of data has become an increasingly complex task.

For beginners stepping into the realm of Natural Language Processing (NLP), one crucial aspect to master is retrieval models. These models enable us to efficiently locate the relevant "needles in the digital haystack" by leveraging various techniques and algorithms.

Retrieval models essentially work by assigning a relevance score to each document in a collection given a specific query or search term. The models aim to identify the most pertinent documents that align closely with the user's information needs.

There are two notable types of retrieval models commonly used in NLP: Boolean retrieval models and probabilistic retrieval models. Let's delve into each to explore their methodologies and applications.

Boolean retrieval models, founded on the principles of Boolean logic, act as a foundation for information retrieval systems. These models utilize Boolean operators such as 'AND', 'OR', and 'NOT' to combine search terms and narrow down the search results. By creating logical expressions and applying them to the document collection, Boolean models can extract documents matching the user's specified criteria. However, these models have limitations since they do not account for relevance ranking and cannot approximate the user's actual information needs accurately.

On the other hand, probabilistic retrieval models address these limitations by using statistical techniques to estimate relevance scores. One of the most influential probabilistic models is the Vector Space Model (VSM). Surrounded by this model, documents and queries are represented as vectors in a high-dimensional space, with each dimension corresponding to a unique term found in the document collection. The cosine similarity measure is employed to determine the relevance between the query vector and each document vector. By ranking the documents based on their cosine similarity scores, the most relevant documents with respect to the query are retrieved.

Building on the foundation of the VSM, advanced retrieval models such as the Okapi BM25 algorithm have been developed. BM25 accommodates various factors such as term frequency, document length, and document collections, amplifying its precision and recall in comparison to elementary vector space models.

Furthermore, machine learning techniques, particularly neural networks, have also found a place in retrieval models. Deep Learning models like convolutional neural networks (CNN) and recurrent neural networks (RNN) have been employed to capture contextual information and semantic meaning, enabling more nuanced search results.

Effectively utilizing retrieval models requires proficiency in preprocessing techniques like tokenization, stop-word removal, stemming, and clustering. These preprocessing steps aid in streamlining the documents and queries while reducing noise or irrelevant information.

Moreover, to enhance retrieval performance and overcome data sparsity, techniques such as relevance feedback and pseudo-relevance feedback can be employed. These techniques leverage the user's or initial retrieved documents' feedback to iteratively refine and improve the search results.

By understanding and exploring retrieval models, beginners can dive deeper into the field of NLP, harnessing their power to tackle the challenge of finding relevant information in the digital haystack. Continual exploration and research in this evolving field will undoubtedly lead to the development of novel strategies and models that will strengthen information retrieval systems and make them more effective and efficient.

11.4 Evaluating Quests: Assessing Retrieval Expeditions

The realm of Natural Language Processing (NLP) is a vast and ever-evolving field that holds the potential to revolutionize the way humans interact with technology. With the exponential growth of digital data, extracting useful information from unstructured text has become a critical challenge. NLP techniques aim to bridge this gap by employing computational methods to understand, interpret, and generate human language.

One of the fundamental tasks in NLP is question answering, wherein a machine is tasked with reading a question and returning the most relevant answer from a given body of text. This requires an effective retrieval system that can scour vast troves of information and pinpoint the most pertinent details.

A critical phase in the development of an NLP question answering system is evaluating its performance and effectiveness in retrieving accurate answers. This process entails designing and conducting retrieval expeditions, whereby a model is tested against a predefined set of questions and evaluated based on its ability to retrieve relevant information.

Evaluating the effectiveness of retrieval expeditions involves several key factors. First and foremost, it is essential to have a diverse and representative collection of questions that cover a broad range of topics and complexities. This ensures that the strengths and weaknesses of the model are thoroughly assessed.

Furthermore, the design of the evaluation tasks should adhere to specific evaluation metrics that measure the performance of the retrieval system. Metrics like precision, recall, F1 score, and Mean Average Precision (MAP) are commonly employed to gauge the model's ability to retrieve relevant passages of text for a given question.

To ensure the reliability of the evaluations, it is crucial to have a diverse set of annotated answers for the evaluation questions. These annotations serve as ground truth, allowing for objective comparisons between the model's responses and the correct answers identified by human annotators.

Evaluating NLP question answering systems also requires addressing potential biases that might be present in the retrieval expeditions. Biases, both explicit and implicit, can significantly impact the performance of the model as certain subjects or viewpoints may be overrepresented or underrepresented in the available data.

To overcome these biases, careful attention needs to be given to data collection and preprocessing. Choosing diverse and unbiased sources of information and meticulously curating the data can help mitigate these effects and improve the overall performance and fairness of the retrieval system.

Finally, it is essential to contextualize the evaluation results by comparing the performance of the model against existing state-of-the-art techniques. This comparative analysis provides valuable insights into the strengths and limitations of the proposed NLP system and helps with identifying areas for improvement and future research directions.

In conclusion, properly evaluating retrieval expeditions is a crucial step in the development of effective NLP question answering systems. Selecting diverse evaluation questions, employing appropriate evaluation metrics, using annotated ground truth data, mitigating biases in data, and benchmarking against existing models are all fundamental aspects of this evaluation process. By meticulously assessing the model's performance, researchers and developers can make informed decisions and continuously advance the state of the art in Natural Language Processing.